New Library of Pastoral Care
GENERAL EDITOR: DEREK BLOWS

Derek Blows is the Director of the Westminster Pastoral
Foundation and a psychotherapist at University College
Hospital. He is also an honorary canon of Southwark
Cathedral.

Made in Heaven?

Titles in this series include:

New Library of Pastoral Care
GENERAL EDITOR: DEREK BLOWS

MADE IN HEAVEN?

Ministry with those intending marriage

Peter Chambers

First published in Great Britain 1988
SPCK
Holy Trinity Church
Marylebone Road
London NW1 4DU

Acknowledgements

The cartoons on pp. 129 and 133 are reproduced
by permission of *Punch.*

British Library Cataloguing in Publication Data

Chambers, Peter
  Made in heaven? : ministry with those
  intending marriage.
  1. Marriage.   Preparation—Christian
  viewpoints
  I. Title   II. Series
  261.8'3581

  ISBN 0-281-04283-7

Filmset by Pioneer
Printed in Great Britain by
the Anchor Press, Tiptree

Contents

Foreword

The *New Library of Pastoral Care* has been planned to meet the needs of those people concerned with pastoral care, whether clergy or lay, who seek to improve their knowledge and skills in this field. Equally, it is hoped that it may prove useful to those secular helpers who may wish to understand the role of the pastor.

Pastoral care in every age has drawn from contemporary secular knowledge to inform its understanding of man and his various needs and of the ways in which these needs might be met. Today it is perhaps the secular helping professions of social work, counselling and psychotherapy, and community development which have particular contributions to make to the pastor in his work. Such knowledge does not stand still, and a pastor would have a struggle to keep up with the endless tide of new developments which pour out from these and other disciplines, and to sort out which ideas and practices might be relevant to his particular pastoral needs. Among present-day ideas, for instance, of particular value might be an understanding of the social context of the pastoral task, the dynamics of the helping relationship, the attitudes and skills as well as factual knowledge which might make for effective pastoral intervention, and perhaps most significant of all, the study of particular cases, whether through verbatim reports of interviews or general case presentation. The discovery of ways of learning from what one is doing is becoming increasingly important.

There is always a danger that a pastor who drinks deeply at the well of a secular discipline may lose his grasp of his own pastoral identity and become 'just another' social worker or counsellor. It in no way detracts from the value of these professions to assert that the role and task of the pastor are quite unique among the helping professions and deserve to be clarified and strengthened rather than weakened. The theological commitment of the pastor and the appropriate use of his role will be a recurrent theme of the series. At the same time the pastor cannot afford to work in a vacuum. He needs to be able to communicate and co-operate with those helpers in other disciplines whose work may overlap, without loss of his own unique role. This in turn will mean being able to communicate with them through some understanding of their concepts and language.

Finally, there is a rich variety of styles and approaches in pastoral work within the various religious traditions. No attempt will be made to secure a uniform approach. The Library will contain the variety, and even perhaps occasional eccentricity, which such a title suggests. Some books will be more specifically theological and others more concerned with particular areas of need or practice. It is hoped that all of them will have a usefulness that will reach right across the boundaries of religious denomination.

DEREK BLOWS
Series Editor

Preface

There is a growing number of good publications, books and audio-visual aids available to those interested in what is generally called marriage preparation. Many of these are handbooks providing programmes for a series of course sessions and material for leaders to train with and use. There are also several books by American authors which set out in more detail and depth professional practice in pre-marital education and counselling. There is a gap in the middle which this book may help fill.

In this country most couples marrying in church will have a few meetings with their minister beforehand. Here is the basis for a pastoral relationship in which a number of tasks relevant to the needs of the couple can be dealt with. Many ministers want to use this opportunity to support couples and I believe they could do so more effectively, learning step by step from what they are already doing. I hope this book will be of use to those recently ordained, to laypeople with some experience already of leading couples' courses, and to ministers with some years' experience who wish to review what they are doing. A number of exercises and suggested activities are included to provide material for those who would like to use the book for in-service training.

There are many in the Churches who are uncertain about the value of marriage preparation. There are enthusiasts and a lot of new ideas but no solid sense that this or that is what we are meant to be doing. I want to set marriage preparation in a context; I believe this ministry belongs in the ordinary course of life and learning; this time spent mainly before a wedding only makes sense if the Church's ministry is earthed in the ordinariness of family and human relationships. Had there been space I should have liked to have made some links between weddings and the other stages in life in which people are incidentally learning about marriage. So much takes place long before people meet their marriage partners.

I find it easier to meet with a couple than to write about it and still capture the humour and the pleasure of marrying. My personal experience of marriage belongs in Wales and England, and I have little practical knowledge of the cross-cultural patterns familiar to some ministers. It is a side of parochial ministry I have especially enjoyed and I hope something of what I relearned in the Parish of St Michael, Bedminster and from friends and colleagues and training opportunities in Bristol comes to life in these pages. Bishop John Tinsley taught me much and the writings of Dr Jack Dominian along with the Marriage Doctrine Reports provided the stimulus to pursue a long-felt interest.

For the last four years I have enjoyed the benefit of working for the Marriage Education Panel, chaired by the Bishop of St Edmundsbury and Ipswich; I am very grateful to him and to Derek Pattinson, Secretary-General of the General Synod, for allowing me to prepare this book at the same time, and for giving me their personal support. Although the conclusions and opinions are mine, members of the Panel, diocesan family life education officers and many people I have met or worked with, members of various churches and of the main marital agencies, have shared their own expertise and experience generously. In addition to those whose publications I have acknowledged I am grateful to David Rolfe, Margaret Grimer and Joy Thompson for their early view of the landscape, and I thank Richard Craig, John Dennis and Janet Mattinson for reading my first draft and making shrewd and encouraging criticisms. I thank my publishers for their perceptive and well-seasoned advice, and Pauline Druiff who has read my writing, corrected my spelling and been the efficient and forgiving typist. My family have been enthusiastic supporters throughout and I thank them for letting me get on with the task when they might have expected my company.

PETER CHAMBERS
February 1988

Part One

ONE

Meeting

Jeff is twenty-one and Tina is nineteen; they both left school when they were sixteen and they have been going together for three years. They got engaged on Tina's eighteenth birthday and they now plan to get married in eight months' time. Jeff works at a warehouse; Tina works part-time in the catering trade.

They have just called at the vicarage to arrange their wedding. They had arrived a couple of minutes early for the appointment and stood outside wondering whether to press the bell or wait. The vicar saved them the decision (perhaps he had seen them coming); he greeted them cheerfully and let them in. They spent three-quarters of an hour with him and as they walked away from the vicarage they began to talk.

TINA: Well it's booked up now. I'm glad we've got that over. He was all right wasn't he. Not as serious as I thought he was going to be.

JEFF: I wonder what he wants to talk to us about next time. I don't see what he meant when he said that being married is harder than getting married.

TINA: Well, at least he didn't give us a lecture on religion.

JEFF: I hope he's not going to try and put us off; say we're too young or something.

TINA: We've had enough of that from your mum.

John has been the vicar of the parish Tina lives in for five years. He meets couples like Jeff and Tina every year, and does not feel pessimistic about their chances even though they are marrying young. They are a willing pair, trying hard

3

to get things together. Jeff did not have a lot to say but that
does not matter at a first interview; with some encouragement
he would be more forthcoming. Obviously he does not quite
know what to make of priests but he does not seem irreligious,
and would probably say he believed in God. Tina seems the
busy one; she has got it all planned. She is probably quite
shrewd and a good survivor, which is just as well, because
they do not seem to have very much money.

John usually enjoys wedding interviews but wishes he had
a clearer idea about what he is trying to do; there never seems
enough time, but that goes for most things. Sometimes it
would be encouraging to know you have done a good job.

There are three questions here for John:

What am I trying to do?
How do I use my time?
How can I evaluate what I do?

The Task

Suppose John recognises a number of connected tasks:

(i)   to encourage each partner to speak to the other about
      what marriage might mean for them;
(ii) to encourage them to be conscious of the importance of
      the commitment they are making to one another;
(iii) to help them recognise a connection between their
      experience of giving and receiving affection and love,
      and the vows they will make;
(iv) to help them make sense of their wish to be married in
      church using a Christian form of service, and to enjoy
      the occasion.

Those are the aims of someone who believes certain things
about the process of getting married and about his own role
in the process. He believes that engaged partners need to
share their ideas about marriage beforehand and understand
each other's expectations, and that marriage involves a mutual
commitment that has to be consciously expressed. He sees
the marriage service as an occasion for personal ritual set in a
Christian context, in which public words and actions carry
and express private affections. It is important also to consider

the task from another angle. What particular needs might each partner have as an individual and to what extent do they have shared needs as a couple?

When two people want to get married in church often their first concern is to arrange the service. They will expect the minister to help them do this in a competent and friendly way and to treat their decision to marry as seriously as they do themselves. They may be glad of some wise and assured help in dealing with their nervousness or apprehension about the arrangements. What they will probably not be expressing openly at this stage is concern for the strength and depth of their own relationship. Either or both of the partners may be feeling concerned about this, but neither of them is likely to put such feelings into words without some encouragement and the assurance that it is safe to do so. Each partner may have questions to ask and feel that there are things they need to know about, but they may need encouragement to broach them. A minister has to recognise these needs, some expressed and some hidden, in order to make contact with the couple and deal with their agenda.

Time

What time is available for this work and how can it be used? Suppose John reckons that the time spent with each couple adds up to about three and a half hours; with twenty weddings a year that might average out at one and a half hours each working week. From a couple's point of view this amounts to four separate occasions when they have personal contact with the minister. After each meeting a couple will probably talk together about what took place. It will mean a conscious effort and use of their time and some couples would question the amount of time involved, particularly if they see little purpose in it. The minimum amount of time needed is determined by what the couple need to do and the practical and legal duties the minister has to carry out. The maximum amount of time is set by the overall task the minister decides to undertake, consistent with the priority to be given to this work, and the willingness of the couple to set aside that time. They will have to agree to the task.

If the minister has the assistance of other ministers, ordained or lay, or arranges to work with groups of couples together, the total time spent can be shared out and may be reduced. For many ministers the arrangements need to be flexible to allow for open-ended activity which will vary in detail and depth from couple to couple. Can the time be planned in advance? It may require working not to a definite plan of activity but allowing a certain amount of time for conversation in particular areas, and recognising that some couples will respond more easily than others. What can be planned is the time to be set aside for particular meetings or interviews and their sequence. More will often be accomplished through having two short meetings with time in between, than by having one long one. An hour of demanding activity without a break is often long enough.

Evaluation

The third question can now be seen to be a very practical one. If time is to be spent, it will be sensible to know how it can be most effectively used. Let us suppose that John has arrived at a pattern of interviewing that appeals to him and which he regards as comfortable for the couples involved. He seems to be able to pursue the task he has identified, yet at the end of the time does not have any way of recognising whether certain deliberate objectives have been achieved. Nor is he altogether confident that he is doing very well. If, for example, he is trying to engage both partners in conversation, he may need greater skill in facilitating this by using deliberate techniques. It would mean picking up clues early on that will help him to connect with each partner's personal experience.

There will probably be times when little seems to have been achieved and John may have felt very little rapport with some couples by the time of their wedding. At the wedding ceremony he may sometimes feel disappointed about the way the couple or their guests behave and reckon that all the time spent with them beforehand has had little effect. This may be no more than a personal reaction, one of feelings and mood related to how he took the service.

It will be helpful for any minister to recognise what he feels about each couple, their marriage service and how he has played his part. That subjective assessment will be all the better if it is balanced by feedback from the couple and others involved in the wedding. But if the work done is to be evaluated objectively, the minister will also need a theoretical framework which gives sense to particular activities. He has to be able to recognise where he is going and what he is doing, using reliable indicators that show what is happening as conversation, activity and ritual take place.

A minister may consider work of this kind worthwhile because he has other aims that are unstated. Does he hope that his effort may cause some couples to realise that they ought not to get married? If so, would it be seen to be worthwhile if every year a few couples call off their wedding? He may have long-term aims as well as short-term ones, long-term aims that are difficult to measure but are connected with the wish to see more couples making and sustaining lasting and fulfilling marriages. Or he may hope that those who get married will in due course become practising Christians.

It is important to keep a sense of perspective. If a minister is to invite a couple to spend time with him preparing for their marriage in a way they are going to find agreeable, why should he expect them to be greatly changed by the experience? By aiming for too much he may be constantly disappointed and not recognise what has been achieved. By setting realistic objectives to begin with, he is more likely to be able to evaluate what he does and to recognise progress.

Ministry in particular: ministry in general

In considering the questions raised for one minister in particular, some general issues become evident. There is a connection between meeting with couples when they come to get married and ministry at other times in their lives; it is a link that people will make in their own way. Ministers cannot make the connection for them but can respond to the way people do it for themselves. The Church gives a context to many activities and meetings with people at various stages in their life and through the experience of its members and by its ministry it engages with the life cycle. Thus the actions of particular ministers or members of a congregation at a given time and place may make it more or less inevitable that people will see the link between their own circumstances and the visible activity of the Church.

So I may recognise that what I do today when I meet a couple may affect their transactions with another minister in years to come. It also means that the Church's ministry through the life cycle does not require a particular link with the same minister, church or congregation throughout. In a book of this size there is not room to indicate in detail what this could mean in practice when, for example, pastoral opportunities occur during adolescence and young adult life or when parents bring infants to be christened. In the following pages the focus will be on the response to a couple's request to be married in church, but you may wish to make the connections with christenings and youth work.

This focus on a particular ministry will capture just snapshots of men and women at the time they marry. These couples may not be very conscious of what they know about marriage or like what they have seen. Whatever marriage in general may be, when people plan to marry someone specific, they begin to consider their own marriage as a particular event and relationship, somehow unlike any other. Some may not plan very much for it; just drift into it trusting in love and good luck. Some may take their vows seriously and yet have little experience of loving or being loved. There is much that cannot be anticipated in advance or deliberately prepared for, but whatever the particular circumstances, each partner can be seen to have a task to do in getting ready for the event and the relationship of marriage.

The task of those who marry is to prepare themselves physically and mentally, emotionally and spiritually, for making a public commitment to live as a married couple: and to enter further into a secure relationship of sexual and intimate love in which they will be changed and through which they will be challenged to accept changes in each other and in their relationships with other people. They may not be aware of all that in those terms, or want or expect someone else to help them with the task. In each case a minister will have to begin where people are, but before coming to the first meeting and beginning to negotiate what needs to be done, he or she will need some sense of personal role.

I say 'he or she' deliberately at this point, because throughout most of the text I use 'he' alone to refer to someone who may be a man or a woman. I write as an Anglican and I hope that by generally using the word 'minister' I will not prevent those who may be thinking in particular of ordained priests, deacons or pastors from making use of this book. The word also refers to those who are not ordained and share in this ministry. The specific contribution which those who are ordained have to make should become evident by careful consideration of the several ministerial roles that can be exercised. Before examining some of those roles we need to consider another question: What is marriage? Bound up with the roles we adopt and the tasks we undertake will be our view of marriage.

TWO

What is Marriage?

Marriage is given, that husband and wife may comfort and help each other, living faithfully together in need and in plenty, in sorrow and in joy. It is given, that with delight and tenderness they may know each other in love, and, through the joy of their bodily union, may strengthen the union of their hearts and lives. It is given, that they may have children and be blessed in caring for them and bringing them up in accordance with God's will, to his praise and glory.
(The Alternative Service Book 1980)

Institution

Marriage is a human institution, an idea to which people collectively subscribe, and a set of relations regulated in most societies by social, ritual or legal form. Custom or law determines who shall be allowed to marry and prescribes the conditions that have to be fulfilled before a marriage can take place. A man and woman who get married acquire new roles and status as husband and wife, together with rights and responsibilities. There may be no such thing as a 'normal marriage' but the state of being married is supported by convention such that it will be normal for many people to marry and develop recognisable patterns of married life. Marriage is esteemed for conservative reasons because it upholds stability in society. Well-founded marriages can provide a kind of molecular structure holding household and society in a firmly bonded pattern. The relations between men and women in marriage affect the relations between men and women politically in society; social and cultural conventions affect the way in which husbands and wives treat each other.

Men and women in every age have resisted getting married.

Their reasons may have varied but for some marriage will have been unattractive precisely because of the conventions that governed relations between husband and wife. They may, for example, have found deeper and better friendship because they did not marry. There are no clear indications that marriage is likely to cease being a popular human estate in the foreseeable future in the United Kingdom. Its popularity over other forms of household life and sexual union may become less established and well defined; cohabitation in various forms is becoming increasingly a prelude to marriage, but there is as yet no clear statistical evidence that radical alternatives to marriage are acquiring comparable status in this country.

Questions about the future of marriage are not resolved simply by evidence that people will go on getting married. What is needed is more than a widely-held belief that marriage is a good thing if it happens to work out; it is the persistence of marriage as a lifelong commitment for which people are willing to make moral choices. The motivation to do that will derive more from what men and women learn by experience than from what they are told. To many of them it is not self-evident that fulfilment in sexual and domestic activity follows from a life-long and monogamous commitment in marriage.

Once a marriage has been legally contracted, it has a public status which cannot be set aside privately by the partners themselves. The law makes provision for divorce because it is evident that some marriages do not last in the way that society and the individual partners had intended. In the United Kingdom the extent of marriage breakdown is now de-stabilising what have been accepted patterns of family life. Nevertheless there is evidence that most people who seek divorce regard it as a drastic step which they do not take lightly.

Relationship

A man and a woman who marry may be hoping for a continuing relationship of love, marked by mutual happiness and sustained by shared affection. Such a union can take on an identity of its own which gives meaning to their life together and to each of them as separate persons. They become committed friends and intimate life companions, each trusting and relying on the other.

Outwardly the relationship has recognisable features; it is a mutual society, organised with varying degrees of informality often determined by class and culture. In their marriage each partner may exercise different roles; some roles may be interchangeable or shared whereas others may seem to belong to one or other partner quite distinctly according to sex. It is likely that some roles will be conventionally assumed by husband or wife without question until a crisis, handicap or illness or economic circumstances compel a change of habit.

The marriage relationship is a sexual one in two senses. Firstly, husband and wife are conscious of being of different sex. In any friendship or working partnership of men and women, individuals may become more aware of what it is to be male and to be female. In a close relationship these perceptions may be questioned and changed. Marriage offers an intimacy and privacy in which sexuality may be experienced securely. Partners continue to be man and woman but they learn new ways of being so, and of acting with deeper love and integrity. Each may become more aware of personal feelings and deeply-held convictions and be able to express them in a variety of ways, no longer governed simply by conventions about how a man or a woman is supposed to behave. At first these changes may be evident only within the privacy of marriage and the family, but in the course of time become more apparent socially as a person grows confident about them.

Secondly, marriage carries an expectation that a husband and wife will want sexual intercourse, and the bond can secure the conditions in which it is to be most richly experienced. Yet it is a fact that those conditions are sometimes found outside marriage, and not always within it. Making love means more than just an exciting and invigorating transitory experience; it affects the emotions in a deep and changing way. Men and women may control the degree to which they remain separate individuals or become involved with one another; lovemaking changes the balance between separation and incorporation. The desire to become physically united with another person will encourage intercourse; and the wish to remain apart will discourage it. Partners may need to learn from each other how to recognise and respect these changes of mood and desire.

To make love is to give adoration. The sensations enjoyed may be familiar in worship and prayer: ecstacy, deep intimacy with another and tranquil peace. The acceptance of each by the other and the continually renewed mutual commitment and thanksgiving implicit and explicit in lovemaking, conversation and shared life together are elements in what could be called a communion. Both partners may become conscious that their union is centred on God and shared beyond their marriage, so that others may benefit because a husband and wife act together unselfishly in love. Their love can be pro-creative, both in this general sense and through the gift of children.

Procreation

Nine out of ten married couples in this country become parents, bearing or adopting their children. Others will wish to but be unable to have children. And any assumed link between marriage and procreation will be questioned by those who have chosen to be married without children, and by those who choose to conceive and bring up children out of wedlock. Yet the bond of marriage has been generally encouraged in European society because it can offer stability to family and household life, providing the security that is desirable for the nurture and well-being of children. That stability can be evident when two partners are willing and able to organise their lives and devote attention to their children in ways that balance changing needs satisfactorily.

Homelessness and hunger are threats to the welfare of children and household unity so that attitudes to parenting are often closely related to matters of family economy. Historically, in England a concern to provide adequately for the needs of children, has caused couples to delay marriage until they were sufficiently confident that they could maintain themselves. In other parts of the world such as Africa and India, children were themselves the insurance taken out by parents to ensure their welfare in old age. In the richer countries of the world today, the birth and survival of babies has been affected by developments in hygiene and medicine. The greater use of contraception has reduced the number of live births and affected sexual behaviour. The survival of the human race is now threatened much more by factors other than the possibility that all who marry not be fruitful and multiply.

Men and women with particular vocations to fulfil and couples who intend to take part in specific work together, may see the fruits of their love and marriage realised in projects they bring to fulfilment or service they carry out for others. In some cases the decision not to have children will be a deliberate act of sacrifice. Procreation is not merely a biological act; it is a thoughtful and emotional act of will, motivated by love. Biological instincts play their part in the care and nurture of children but it is also an activity motivated by the mind and emotions, and, consciously or unconsciously, it is a spiritual vocation. Those who have adopted or fostered children are continuing a pattern of childrearing seen all through history.

In each generation a mother and father may, knowingly or otherwise, recall and re-enact their own family story and parent-and-child experience as each responds to the experience of being a parent and making a family life anew. Habits and patterns that are called forth by this experience may be mutually endorsed or may cause the partners to come into conflict with one another. They may modify what they have received from the past with the result that new habits and patterns of family life are formed. Any picture of the joys and pains of family life may be very particular. Some parents, for example, may find it impossible to imagine that children can be abused or assaulted by their own parents; yet we know this happens and is often kept secret by the loyalties and privacy that in other circumstances are rightly protected.

The procreation of children is full of hope; it is a risk taken in love. Children may die, become ill or remain constantly dependent on their parents. Their presence will affect, and may cause stress in, the relationship between husband and wife. There will be economic as well as personal sacrifices to be made. Some children may reject in different ways the love of their parents; they may disrupt or bring trouble to family life. When children grow up, even when they marry, they may continue to demand much of their original family and still cause their parents joy and pain. Parents whose marriages end in divorce after their children have come of age may discover that their children still needed their marriage more than any of them had realised.

A sacred union

Marriage as an honourable human estate; marriage as the love of a man and a woman; marriage as the basis for family life: these are three aspects or dimensions that also contain a fourth. Marriage is a holy and sacred covenant; the sexual instincts and parental sentiments already described are God-given. Such a conviction may dawn slowly or not at all through a person's experience of family affection and marital love. A couple making love may experience in their tenderness for one another a profound sense of thankfulness and blessing. As their affection increases and is deepened, each partner may experience in his and her own way a conviction that their union has been brought about by God. Their love is not merely an exciting passion but is held by a commitment that is binding and unbreakable; its human quality is transcended and they know it is 'for ever and ever, Amen'. For either to end it, would be to break a sacred trust.

The sense of the sacred may also come through the ordinariness of family life. This may be seen in a couple who have a mature way of dealing with the expectations a lively household places upon them and who make it clear that they have a life of their own too; partners who know each other as well as they know themselves, who know how to give affection, do battle and restore the image in each other; a couple glad to share themselves with family and friends; each will have reason to give thanks for the past, rejoice in the present and trust God for the future.

Marriage, as a sacred union, embraces the other three facets of marriage: the institutional, the relational, and the familial. No attempt has been made here to separate the sacred from the secular although that is what many today would wish to do. The way all three of those facets or dimensions are viewed can cause men and women to recognise that their experience transcends human language and ceremonies. In their sentiments for their children and their duty as parents, in their affection and dependence on one another as partners, and in their regard for the order and calling of marriage itself, they experience the love of God and divine order. They 'mime'[1] the mystery of 'Christ and the Church'.

Views of marriage

The view that has just been outlined is a commentary on the way marriage has been perceived in Christian tradition. It is provided as one kind of answer to the general question, 'What is marriage?'. Each person may come to a view of marriage which is to some extent formed from their own experience and is to some extent inherited from tradition. What has been borrowed may in time be returned or passed on to others, duly shaped by experience. This is a theme to which I shall return in the final chapter but for the moment it will be useful to see how people's different insights can be discovered through a simple educational exercise.

Imagine one to two dozen men and women of various ages who have come together for a discussion about marriage. One or two are unmarried, others have been divorced or widowed but most are married. Discussion begins in groups of threes. One person in each group is given a few minutes to talk without interruption about marriage as he or she sees it. A few more minutes are then allowed for the other two in the group to ask questions to draw out points referred to. After this a second person takes a turn as speaker, and then the third. The leader then invites everyone together to take up some of the points already talked about in the threesomes.

This soon becomes a lively debate with little unanimous agreement. When the leader points this out, one person suggests some matters people are agreed on, and gets some support. Another person objects to that and says that there is no point in pretending that everyone is agreed when they aren't. 'In the end it all comes down to personal experience; why do we all have to be the same anyway?' she says. The leader responds by asking her to say a bit more about what she feels. Someone else then says that they feel very strongly that the Church often wants to put people into tidy compartments like 'happily married', 'single', or 'divorced'. She has felt for some time that she doesn't belong in any of these compartments. Several other people add comments and the leader concludes by inviting everyone in turn to repeat, if they want to, one thing they are glad to have heard said or have been able to say during the session.

Such an exercise might only have generated conversation that was guarded and fairly tentative; there would have been considerable resistance to being honest and to presenting personal experience. People taking part might have tried to prevent disagreement and the leader might have deliberately encouraged this by preventing people from expressing and sharing personal feelings.[2]

When some of the natural resistance to sharing and learning can be overcome, that sort of exercise can be very useful as a way of enabling individuals to recognise how much personal experience has shaped their attitudes to marriage. Those who believe they do not know much about marriage may soon discover that they do have ideas and even strongly held convictions. They may also discover that they are able to understand a great deal about marital relations. Yet the resistance may be considerable. Men and women who have not married may be discouraged from sharing their insights because others have assumed they have no experience. Those who are married may find it hard to acknowledge their own experience, particularly if it has been unhappy or painful.

As a further aid to reflection or as a discussion starter in an exercise such as that just described, one of the following questionnaires may be useful. The first is based on material derived from the European Study of Values begun in the early 1980s. It deals with thirteen different items that may be thought to contribute, to a greater or lesser extent, to the making of a successful marriage. The task of ranking the items can stimulate group discussion. A key based on the results of the Values Study is also provided for information, and would be distributed to participants after discussion has already created some interest. If you are simply using the list for your own interest, carry out the ranking before looking at the key.

The second questionnaire is based on experience from a number of discussion groups in different places; those taking part should complete it on their own before entering into discussion. It can provoke personal reflection and lead them to a clearer understanding of their own knowledge of marriage. By asking a group to reach consensus agreement, participants can be encouraged to recognise the strength and importance of personal convictions.

Discussion starters

Exercise 1: Factors that contribute to a successful marriage

Number the following in the order in which you think they are most important. Number the most important 1, and the least important 13.

- . . . Faithfulness
- . . . Adequate Income
- . . . Sharing same social background
- . . . Mutual respect
- . . . Sharing religious beliefs
- . . . Good housing
- . . . Sharing political views
- . . . Understanding and tolerance
- . . . Living apart from in-laws
- . . . Happy sex relations
- . . . Sharing household chores
- . . . Having children
- . . . Sharing tastes and interests in common

(Derived from *Values and Social Change in Britain*, ed. M. Abrams, D. Gerard and N. Timms (Macmillan 1985).)

For information after discussion: These factors are next set out in the order in which they were ranked in the British Values Study.[3]

PERSONAL
1. Faithfulness
2. Mutual respect and appreciation
3. Understanding and tolerance
4. Happy sex relations

BACKGROUND
5. Living apart from in-laws
6. Having children
7. Tastes and interests in common
8. Good housing
9. Adequate income
10. Sharing household chores

CULTURAL
11. Sharing same social background
12. Sharing religious beliefs
13. Sharing political views

Exercise 2: What is essential for a comfortable and lasting marriage?

This is a simple questionnaire that can be used in a number of ways. If several people complete it and then compare their answers it can provoke interesting discussion, particularly if they are then asked to reconsider and agree on their choices.

Put a tick opposite each of the statements that you think would rank among the most important conditions for a comfortable and lasting marriage.

1. The marriage vows were made in church
2. Neither spouse had slept with anyone else before marriage
3. Both partners want children
4. Both partners have a sense of humour
5. As a couple they make love regularly
6. Both partners share similar beliefs and attitudes
7. Each partner has other close friends
8. Each partner is faithful to the other sexually
9. Each partner trusts the other
10. Both partners are willing to accept change in each other

11. As a couple they are agreed on, and able to provide for, essential needs of housing, clothing and food
12. Both partners are agreed about their roles as husband and wife
13. Each partner is capable of showing forgiveness
14. Each partner is able to give and receive affection
15. Both partners can deal fairly in disagreements and rows
16. Both partners are prepared to put their marriage before any other commitment
17. . . . .
    (add your own if you wish)

When you have worked right through the list, if there is time, think again, and put the six most important statements in rank order from 1 to 6.

Notes

1. The word is used by Tinsley, E. J. in *The Imitation of God in Christ* (SCM Press 1960) when discussing Ephesians 5.25−33.
2. There is not space in this volume to go into detail about ways of leading groups; there is some suggested reading in the Notes following Chapter 7.
3. This is the ranking given in 1985 based on a survey in 1981. In 1987, a further publication, *British Social Attitudes* (Gower 1987) reported the results of a 1985 survey in which the order of ranking changed slightly (1981 ranking in brackets): 1. Faithfulness (1); 2. Mutual respect and appreciation (2); 3. Understanding and tolerance (3); 4. Living apart from in-laws (5); 5. Happy sexual relationship (4); 6. Adequate income (9); 7. Good housing (8); 8. Having children (6); 9. Sharing household chores (10); 10. Tastes and interests in common (7); 11. Sharing same social background (11); 12. Shared religious belief (12); 13. Agreement on politics (13).

THREE

Rite and Roles

The word marriage refers both to the state of being married and to the ceremony of marrying. At a wedding those present seem to be giving public support not only to the couple marrying but also to the institution. The couple marrying are seen as a sign that marriage will survive: the hope that their marriage will survive is supported by the ceremony. Among the guests there may be some who have regrets about their own marriage mingled with good hopes for the bride and groom; and there will be others for whom the celebration resonates with gratitude for their own wedded happiness. In much of Europe including the British Isles, the earliest forms of Christian office at a marriage would have consisted of prayers and blessings at home. Only from the eleventh century did it become more common in England for these ministrations to take place in church and later at the altar.

Why marry in church?

Church marriage has never been universal in this country, although the passing of Lord Hardwicke's Marriage Act in 1753, which was intended to stop clandestine marriages, came near to encouraging it. For over eighty years after it was promulgated until provision was made in 1836 for civil registration the only way to become legally married, unless you were a Quaker or a Jew, was in church. It did for the Church of England what the decree of the Council of Trent did in the Roman Catholic Church. Yet couples, probably unconcerned about property rights, still came together without 'benefit of clergy'. For centuries the Church had recognised the *de facto* status of unions made without parental approval and priestly blessing, provided the couple themselves had

properly given their consent. Thus the Church law of Western
Europe which replaced Roman law provided the modern
basis on which the consent of the couple expressed in vows of
marriage has become the heart of the marriage ceremony.
Although not everyone has married in church, the development of the Church's services has shaped the way in which
men and women have gone about the process of getting
married. The popular view was well illustrated at the last two
royal weddings in London. The words of bride and groom
expressing their willingness to marry were relayed to the
waiting crowds who responded with loud cheers.

Whereas 150 years ago the greater proportion of church
weddings involved the better-off, more recently those who
have married in church have come from a much wider cross-
section of society. But for this redistribution there might have
been a much sharper decline in the proportion of weddings in
church. In the late 1950s the importance attached to 'proper'
weddings by those for whom increasing prosperity and
respectability went hand in hand, ensured that nearly three-
quarters of all ceremonies were in church or chapel.[1] Those
sentiments strongly persist in the minds of parents and
grandparents and are transmitted to the next generation.
Conventions that apply to major life events change more
slowly than everyday ways of behaving, partly because those
events call for resources outside a person and draw on the
wisdom of the past.

A person may feel under some obligation to be married in
church; one partner may be doing it for the sake of the other,
or both could be doing it to please their parents. They may be
responding to an indefinable sense of propriety. Someone
who sincerely believes they ought to be married in church
because it is the proper way to do it may not understand a
minister who cannot recognise that. 'Why do you want to be
married in church?', is a question that is often out of order; it
does not fit the context. It could be rather like asking a
football supporter why he supports his home team. Yet it is a
question that ministers often ask. Perhaps a priest who takes
very few weddings because most couples opt for the register
office is genuinely curious and considers it a sensible starting
point. What is more likely is that a clergyman in asking the

question is expressing some confusion about what he is doing marrying people who do not come to church. A couple who want to marry may be asking for three things: a ceremony to make them married, a place at which to be married, and an official to marry them. How do these expectations fit what the Church provides?[2]

Wanting it done 'rite'

In a primitive sense a rite is some ordained action which men and women carry out in order to ensure their preservation and the promise of divine blessing. This suggests in the case of marrying that a couple have to perform certain actions which constitute their rite, in order to secure their marriage. They also dress for the occasion and they are reinforced by supporters—bridesmaids and a best man. The costumes and the customs have become part of the performance of the rite. The rite exists so that people can handle a transition that is potentially alarming. On the face of it, it seems strange to say that marrying someone you are 'in love with' can be an alarming experience. The most alarming thing about it might appear to be the ceremony itself: a public ordeal to be gone through as quickly as possible.

Here it is apparent that a couple do not simply choose to undergo this ceremony; they are somehow required to make use of it. It apparently exists for the sake of families and the communities from which and into which they are marrying. It marks out what a couple are doing and impresses on them the responsibilities they are acquiring by their change of status. The new status is generally accompanied by changes of domicile and a reordering of close relations with family and friends. The rite is to enable a couple to make this passage from being single to being married and to be effective the ceremony has to take place publicly in the presence of their families and friends.

Family patterns, class and culture have affected the social aspects of the marriage rites and it is worth recognising the hidden messages these convey about the meaning of marriage. The most obvious features reveal something of the notion 'It's the bride's day'. The way a woman is regarded and expects to

be treated has been captured in the ceremony as she makes
the transition from being one man's daughter to another
man's wife. Bridal customs have reinforced the primarily
domestic and maternal roles of women in marriage, a sense
which the Western Church's rites of marriage also preserved
in the prayers derived from the medieval Roman nuptial
blessings. The use or not of the word 'obey' in the marriage
vows is the detail that often draws comment while the
surrounding ritual is taken for granted. Nowadays it is clear
that many brides will want to resist any associations with
being the second sex, but probably as many others will find
the ritual confirms what they have learned from their mothers.
Fashions can be misleading. The white bridal gown began to
become fashionable about two hundred years ago and its
association today is not so much with a woman's presumed
virginity as with the wish to marry beautifully and with style.

The convention of the big wedding is now being rejected by
some men and women for whose parents it was beyond
question. Many of them may be questioning not just the style
but the model of marriage they received from their parents. In
the last twenty years the couple has become a much more
exalted relationship throughout society and those who marry
today are more likely than their parents were to aspire to the
companionate idea of married life. This not just a twentieth-
century fashion. The social history of English marriages
shows it to be characteristic of many unions in past centuries
where wife and husband together managed the household
economy and supported one another with enduring affection.[3]
Those today for whom that is an ideal will seek fulfilment
much more in the quality of their relationship than in having
respectable married status. They may also be resisting a
convention which they believe perpetuates the hypocrisy of
empty-shell marriages and the caricature of holy deadlock.

The status of marriage

Today it is not as clear as it was in earlier generations how a
person's status changes on marriage. The importance and
distinctiveness of marriage has been eroded partly because
the family responsibilities associated with it are no longer

clearly defined or exercised and partly because more people are contracting long-term couple relationships that are comparable to marriage but not quite the same thing. Two people who get married may already feel a committed couple and be used to being treated as one. Being a couple implies some mutual investment in each other; that perception has in the past helped to sustain marriage as an institution. Yet the definition has not always been as clear as we might like to believe. In past centuries couples in a stable relationship living as a household with their children were often considered married even when they had not participated in any formal church rites. They were presumed married by mutual consent and common repute, as they can still be in Scotland. The phrase 'common law marriage', though legally meaningless, provides for the social acceptance of many relationships which have that long-term stability about them.

Increased longevity has extended the meaning of 'lifelong' but rising divorce rates have eroded the sense that marriage has a characteristic permanence. Higher expectations of the happiness and quality of sexual relationships, increasing support for ideas of individual freedom, social mobility and women's emancipation have now had a combined effect on the mechanisms that in recent times kept marriages intact. In this country a fifth of all young adults may have seen their parents' marriages dissolved. This may not have diminished their own wish or inclination to be married, but it may dispose them to be cautious about committing themselves. They may also lack some intuitive understanding of how to be effective marriage partners. Certainly there is growing evidence that more couples are delaying marriage by living together first. At present more than a quarter of women who get married (and have not previously been married) live with their partners before marrying them, on average for a couple of years.[4] This is an option that seems to be most attractive to those working away from home and to those who moved out of their parents' home before they were twenty. Couples who do live together often try to hide the fact, particularly from their parents, and may show in various ways that they are not comfortable about being thought to be 'living in sin'.

The extent to which couples may want to declare what they

are doing will often depend on how much they want their behaviour acknowledged and accepted by others. Some who wish to defy convention or prefer to ignore it may deliberately choose not to be married and find other ways of asking people to recognise their relationships and their assumed status. In social terms getting married means a change of status. How important that change is reckoned to be will depend on the status that is given to marriage. A couple who wish to marry may want their marriage to be confirmed by an institution that is seen to give it status. The Church through its rites and ceremonies may be thought to be doing that in a way that the State is not, even though all marriages registered conform to the same law. In different ways couples may know that there is more to a church wedding than just having 'a nice day'. And the Church gives status to marriage not so much by its contemporary general moral statements but because in diverse times and places it continues to endorse this 'honourable estate' as it celebrates people's marriages.

The person in the rite

In emphasising the social aspects of getting married, the psychological dimensions have simply been hinted at. A person who takes on a new role and status may be presumed to have developed sufficiently to bear the attendant responsibilities. In practical terms, if marriage is combined with setting up a new independent household, partners need to know they are ready for it. But there are emotional adjustments to be made too. The intimacy inherent in marital relations may threaten independence and a person's sense of separateness. Physical departure from home may be a major step in displacing commitment and attachment to parents and childhood friends. The disruption of work and leisure activities may contribute to a sense of insecurity and unease.

The act of marrying is a pivotal moment, a discontinuity, and a person may need a ritual that is secured outside them to provide a way through the transition. At other times in a person's life home and parents may have provided this security, but at this point mothers and fathers have their own task to undertake, that of releasing their children. Another parent is needed and there is a sense in which the Church, through the trio of place, rite and minister, provides that parenting. It has to be given in a manner that is emptied of possessiveness and authoritarianism, for in the end it has to confirm the spouses in their capacity to parent as well as partner each other. If this is what a person is hoping for when they marry in church then clearly the ministry they receive has to confirm them in the knowledge that in marrying in the eyes of God they are becoming married in their own mind.

The minister will do well to hold together what he does as a person with what is provided by the rite. Too strong a sense of personal ministry will obscure the ritual action; too mechanical a use of the rite will inhibit personal participation. To take part means to be caught up in a dynamic process so that what is within a person, both conscious and unconscious, can be given form by symbols, words and ceremonies. The integrity of the rite provides security and impels movement, releasing a person's energy to allow change and trans-formation.[5] The ritual provides a conceptual framework and tools with which a person can recreate or redefine their world. The ceremonies provide the means to act on and make personal what is external. So people come through the ceremony and carry away within them a new sense of who they are. All this is not completed in one short service; the transition takes time and people need to learn how to repeat their rites, not just formally, possibly by coming to a service of renewal of vows, but informally and privately. At the time of marrying, the Church's ministry can enable the couple to perceive that their vows can be recollected in their moments of coming together throughout their life.

One of the functions of the minister is to work towards realising the resources the partners themselves have to be ministers. In Christian understanding the bride and groom are technically the ministers of their rite of marriage. They could prepare their own service and lead it, which, allowing for legal requirements, is sometimes what happens, where Church discipline allows it. Yet most couples who come to get married rely on the officiating minister to provide the service, solemnise the marriage and preside over the celebration in a dignified and benevolent way. In attending to a couple's request to be married in church, a minister is obliged to begin by accepting this role of officiant and with it the responsibility for conducting a proper service. Not everyone finds the obligation congenial; some ministers may feel angry at times about being used by people who want a big wedding. When a minister meets a couple it will not help them or him if he feels trapped in a role he does not wish to exercise. Such feelings have to be acknowledged, but at such time as they can be adequately expressed and dealt with without venting them on the couple. A minister is more likely to respond effectively and generously to what a couple are asking for when he is not distracted by the clamour of his own annoyance and frustration.

What do the couple want? It is not always clear because they may not know themselves what to expect or what is expected of them. Each may have questions to ask and each may expect to be told things they need to know. In some measure they may be aware that they have an underlying task which is more than the sum of all the practical details concerned with arranging their wedding. Above all they have roles to play and they are likely to want to play their parts well. They have to believe in themselves and in the plans they are making. Part of the performance of getting married is showing everyone you can do it, in other words conveying that you are capable and in charge. There is an element of theatre here that is vital. If marriage itself can be thought of as the drama of the man-woman relationship, then the wedding may be a 'curtain-up' with all the principal players coming on stage together for the first time.

The minister may discover he is actor-director-stage manager but his principal task is to help the other players discover and gain confidence in their roles. He won't help the couple if he diminishes their performance by taking charge of both the ceremony and the marriage process and encouraging the couple to feel subject to him in some way. They have their own lines and actions: the officiant's job is to secure the stage and the setting and his other ministerial roles are concerned with rehearsing the players.

More than one role

The role of officiant may include those statutory functions that would in some cases be carried out by an authorised person or registrar. His responsibility is to ensure that the marriage fulfils the conditions laid down and is properly registered. But there is more than that. The minister is an enabler and to be that he will have to marry a number of roles he performs at other times and places to the specific needs of each couple. A man and woman making the transition into marriage may be helped if they are conscious of who they are, where they have come from, and where they hope they are going. Much of that may be very clear to them but it is possible that they will need to find their way and be glad of some support in doing it. It is a task for which a minister familiar with the counselling role (not just in the plain sense of advising) may be well-equipped. It would mean being able to help both partners to reflect on their experience of relationships and decision to marry, without making the counselling task overtly problem-centred.

Because the Church still secures for many people the status of marriage, it may be thought to have something to teach about marriage and ministers are often urged to undertake that educational task with renewed insight and vision. By and large it is a task best done experientially rather than didactically. They will carry into their relations with couples their sense of being ministers of the Church and gospel and quite naturally they will be glad when this evokes some response, but it is a mission to be carefully matched to the partners' own aspirations and beliefs. The more attentive we can be to the faith that is in others, the wiser we may become in travelling with couples on this part of their journey. As ministers we may have to carry, with hope and charity, the difference between the faith of the Church and what couples are able to believe and say.

There are three overlapping tasks: reviewing the decision to marry, learning about marriage and celebrating marriage. By being aware of the minister's distinct roles in the context of this particular ministry and by not confusing them we may be better able to see what we are doing. In practice we may move from one role to another without confusion as long as we mark the boundaries and have the couple's agreement. We shall need to gain their co-operation; we may seek agreement to a series of meetings or a course at our first meeting. Before considering that first step in more detail it may be helpful to refer briefly to the roles that are now recognisable, before dealing with them separately and in more detail in later chapters.

An *officiating minister* assists the couple in the rite of their marriage, meeting their requests as the provisions of the Church allow and taking the service.

A *registrar* has a duty to ensure the prescribed legal requirements are fulfilled and the marriage is properly registered.

A *counsellor* remembers that *he* is not responsible for the couple's decision to marry (*they* are) but may be able to help them to reflect upon and review that decision. He is not the judge of their behaviour in the past; he is one they may wish to talk to about their experience.

A *teacher* has the knowledge and the skill to enable others to learn; he is someone who may be able to help the couple understand more of marriage and become more resourceful in the way they develop and sustain their relationship. He may be able to share this role with others, and by helping the couple prepare the celebration, he may strengthen their roles, their intentions and their knowledge of God.

A *pastor*, after the example of Christ, is a servant of God's love in supporting people in family and marriage as need and opportunity arises.

Notes

1. Statistics can be found in the annual publications of the Office of Population Censuses and Surveys (OPCS), published by HMSO. For further background see Leonard, D., *Sex and Generation*, Tavistock 1980; 'A Proper Wedding' by the same author in Corbin, M., ed., *The Couple*, Penguin 1978; and Gillis, J. R., *For Better, For Worse*, Oxford University Press 1985.
2. Those familiar with Carr, W., *Brief Encounters*, SPCK 1985, will recognise that he has provided a cogent explanation of much of the

process and the minister's role within it. What follows is not an attempt to rewrite that explanation, but for the sake of continuity I find it necessary to cover some of the same ground, albeit less rigorously.

3. See e.g. Macfarlane, A., *Marriage and Love in England 1300—1840*, Blackwell 1986, and Sarsby, J., *Romantic Love and Society*, Penguin 1983. Also Mace, D. and V., *The Sacred Fire*, Nashville, TN: Abingdon 1986.

4. The figure is a conservative estimate based on material obtained from the General Household Survey and published in Social Trends 1987, HMSO.

5. A thorough treatment of this idea of an oscillation process is provided by Reed, B. D., in *The Dynamics of Religion*, Darton, Longman and Todd 1978. It is outlined briefly in Reed, B. D., *Values to Live by: A Study of dependence*, Grubb Institute 1985.

Part Two

FOUR

Beginning

The first meeting creates impressions; a couple are likely to enquire about getting married at the time when they go public about their intentions. The response they get will begin to determine how important for them any involvement with the Church is going to be. Their first experience may be of the ease or difficulty they have in finding out where their local church is and who they have to contact about their wedding arrangements. Local hearsay may be inefficient or even misleading. Unless they are members of the church they may not know anyone in the congregation to ask. Clear information, well displayed on a noticeboard, is wanted. Usually the couple will decide how much in advance of the wedding they make contact. Since it will generally be helpful to see them as soon as possible, the minister may have to be flexible as well as business-like in arriving at a mutually acceptable date and time. There are two practical questions to be considered; what should the meeting be used for and where should it take place?

At this first meeting the minister and the two partners may all wish to create good impressions; indeed the minister may be more keen to do so than the couple. With the best of intentions he will want to begin on the right foot and gain the couple's confidence. Yet it is so easy to start wrong-footed if he is rushing from another appointment to meet them, pre-occupied with something else or if he is immediately unsettled by the way one or both of them behave or by something they say. If one purpose of this first encounter is to establish rapport the meeting will need to be paced and not rushed. The aim might be to gain the couple's trust so that they may have confidence in themselves and the minister. They will need to relax without letting go of their own purpose in coming; the minister's welcome will need to break some of the ice without diverting attention from the task in hand. The agenda is the couple's conscious preparation for getting married, and at this early stage the minister can provide some demonstration of what the Church is offering to that process.

Formalities

Certain formalities have to be dealt with and the minister who has an official role will need to be clear as to what those functions are. All marriages have to be solemnized and registered according to the requirements of the Marriage and Registration Acts, and the Registrar General issues booklets for the guidance of clergy and authorized persons. About 110,000 marriages a year are dealt with entirely by the clergy of the Church of England, and a further 50,000 by 'authorized persons', ministers and others who conduct the marriage ceremony and register the marriage but do not deal with the preliminaries. Unless a marriage is to take place by Licence, which can usually be obtained at short notice, twenty-one days notice is needed by a superintendent registrar for the issue of a certificate, and effectively four Sundays' notice for the calling of banns by clergy. In practice couples generally allow more time than that in order to be sure of making arrangements. Apart from an expectation that couples will show courtesy in planning ahead, some churches have further rules about a minimum time: six months, for example, may be stipulated. The more time there is, the less the minister will be constrained to deal simply with the formalities.

The information provided by the partners has to be truthful. Some of it determines whether they are entitled to marry (age, present marital status, close kindred or affinity), some of it may determine where they can be married (address, church membership status) and some of it the status which their marriage may subsequently have (nationality, religious affiliation). A minister may not be able to check some of this information for himself and if he has good reason to doubt the honesty of either of the partners, or the accuracy of what they tell him, he may wish to consult competent Church authorities or the local superintendent registrar. Some of the information given by the prospective spouses has to be accurately recorded in the marriage registers at the time of the marriage. Names have to be correctly spelt and ages and addresses correctly given. At the preliminary stage these details have to be checked and legibly written out. Any doubt about spelling of names, the identity of a person's father or how any change of name should be noted will usually have to be raised at this stage in a way that does not encourage alarm. These are not details that can prevent people marrying, but they ensure that the wedding register and any copies of the entry are correct, which may prevent difficulties later. The minister's role in this respect is as important as any other, and ensuring the efficiency of necessary bureaucratic procedures is as much for the couple's sake as for anyone else's. The Registrar General's notes of guidance will often provide the answer to unusual questions and it is worth having an up-to-date copy.

Does the officiant at the wedding have to be the person who deals with the formalities? Local circumstances will often determine the answer but a few points are worth considering. The information that is needed for the registers becomes public at the wedding so in that sense it is not confidential. Some of the enquiries may however touch on matters of illegitimacy or divorce about which people may be naturally reticent. Occasionally the unreliability of information may be sensed only by an experienced interviewer. Whoever makes the enquiries and gathers the information, it is still the officiating minister who takes responsibility for the procedures having been properly carried out. If one of the partners or witnesses, on seeing the registers, suggests there is an inaccuracy in the written entry, the person who completed it may be needed so that facts can be checked and corrections made. The Registration Act says that entries shall be made in the register after the marriage has been solemnized. If that requirement is to be followed, in the absence of a registrar, ample time has to be allowed for writing up as well as signing the registers, or someone other than the officiant be appointed to do it.

In churches where the office of clerk, or a similar appointment, exists, it might be that person's job to deal with the registration details as distinct from the preliminary enquiries, provided there is a clear understanding about who does what, and a safe procedure for handing on information. If that person were also expected to deal with the preliminary enquiries, together with booking the wedding dates and answering all the questions couples might want to ask, he or she would in effect be carrying out the first interview. In team ministries different people may take turns to be on duty. Then it is essential for any arrangements for first interviews to take realistic account of the needs, expectations and apprehensions of the couples. Whoever meets them first has to be in a position to represent the Church adequately and warmly and have the authority to book dates and deal with practical questions. If too much is deferred the couple may be left feeling uncertain and feel they are being passed on down the line instead of being dealt with personally.

Here then are some of the basic tasks that need to be addressed at a first interview:

— welcoming the couple and showing them a willingness to assist them in their process of becoming married;
— obtaining the information needed to ensure the partners are legally entitled to marry and qualified to do so in the church they have chosen;
— explaining to the couple the procedures and further formalities they will have to deal with before the wedding can take place and ensuring that these are done;
— dealing with particular questions the couple want to ask;
— explaining any information they are given about facilities the Church offers to those getting married including arrangements that concern the service.

The last item may be deferred to a later occasion. The couple may not raise all the questions on their mind at a first interview.

The setting for the interview

Ideally two conditions have to be met. The minister needs to have certain information and paperwork to hand and may want to refer to dates and directories. The couple should not be unduly inhibited or distracted by surroundings that may inevitably be unfamiliar or feel strange. Some people feel more comfortable doing business collaboratively around a table and others can feel at ease in an easy chair facing the person they are dealing with. Partners will probably prefer being close enough to consult and may be apprehensive about someone writing down things about them which they cannot see. Ministers who wish to provide flexibility often arrange separate chairs and a settee in a room to allow people to choose what is most comfortable, and then seat themselves in the most convenient position afterwards. If people are likely to arrive early or while the minister is occupied with something else, a comfortable place to wait will be needed.

The two obvious locations are likely to be at the church, possibly in a vestry, office or small room in a hall, or at the minister's own home. The church may seem more business-like and more like neutral ground than someone's home and would be convenient if the couple wished to go into the church itself to see what it is like. At home a minister may be able to offer more comfortable hospitality and sometimes more privacy. Something of his own personality and domestic circumstances would be conveyed by the furnishings, background noise and glimpses of those who share his home. He should consider if this is what he wants as a basis for the working relationship he intends to develop.

Beyond the formalities

This first meeting may also mark the beginning of a pastoral relationship which will in some cases continue well into a couple's marriage. It may be important for the couple to meet the person who is likely to be taking their wedding, as far as that can be known. Simply by meeting the person they perceive to be in charge they may be reassured that they are going to be personally looked after. This can be appropriate and helpful at this stage and a minister may do well not to resist this dependence upon him; there will be an opportunity to hand over some of the responsibility later. Where does the timing of this meeting fit into the development of each couple's own relationship? Clearly they are not yet married in law but they may already know they are wed to each other in their own hearts and minds. A wedding is a public event in the intimate and social process of becoming married, but for the partners it may seem an artificial event designed more to meet the aspirations of their family and friends. The minister may be uncertain where this private relationship has got to, but he will be aware that the public event is likely to affect their intimate and personal life in ways that may not be foreseen.

At this stage one partner may be more committed to the relationship than the other; one may be more certain than the other that he or she wants to be married. Such a disparity may be more obvious to an outsider than it is to the partners themselves and it can mean that the business of planning the wedding is not based on a deliberate decision that they are equally committed to. Some difference of commitment is to be expected and, unless it is clearly very one-sided, is not necessarily a serious problem. This disparity of commitment can be discovered and surveyed obliquely by encouraging each partner in turn to answer any questions the minister asks, deliberately indicating that he does not expect them to be in agreement or to have already made decisions about some of the matters being raised. If the first interview takes place soon after the couple have announced their plans to marry and well before the wedding, they can be encouraged to regard these early months of preparation as an opportunity to live with their ideas of getting married and to recognise what significance this has for them. A minister may suggest at this point that his role could be to help them review their decision to marry and begin to recognise what changes this will bring to their relationship and to their individual ways of life.

Blending the formalities with this further exploration can be helpful. It gets business done without reducing those involved to the roles of enquirers and respondents. If obtaining necessary personal information is to be used as a starting point for indicating some of the other tasks they can engage in, the questions could be asked in an extended and unhurried way. The object would be to encourage personal sharing while allowing each person to determine how much they wish to reveal. To be party to this activity, a minister will have to reveal something of himself in the conversation in a genuine way, sharing personal information naturally without inflicting his life story on the couple. This may require a number of practical steps:

— before filling in any enquiry form the minister shows it to the couple and explains what it is for;
— the minister sits where he can give the same attention to each partner without obvious disparity;
— a few opening questions are addressed to both partners without haste so that they can get used to the minister's manner and gauge how they can talk to him, a prerequisite for safe conversation;
— conversation can be encouraged by responding initially in a non-judgemental way to some of the information given, simply seeking clarification.

Consciously giving attention to both partners may mean not picking up the sad events in one partner's life too quickly, however important they may be, for this can produce an imbalance of attention as the other partner is left out. (Significant events can be explored later when both partners have shown it is appropriate and are ready to consider them together.) The first session should not be prolonged, however interesting it becomes. Forty-five minutes is usually enough and if some information has not been obtained the partners can be asked to provide it at the next session. Each partner should have enough time to raise the questions he or she wants answered even though consideration of it may sometimes be better deferred to another occasion (the minister needs to show he has heard the question and may note it down).

To support this approach a minister will ordinarily need some effective system for recording information and a basis for planning further time with each couple. (A checklist is given in Appendix E.)

FIVE

Establishing Rapport

At the first interview, when there is time to go beyond formalities, a minister has the opportunity to begin to develop a working relationship with a couple and gain their trust. Without this trust there is little point in starting on some of the personal and pastoral tasks that will give a purpose to whatever limited time can be spent together. The process of building trust cannot be rushed, but it can be aided by paying attention to some basic guidelines. By looking at a few illustrations we can recognise what these are. We might take it for granted that for the minister the general aim in establishing rapport would be to learn more about both partners, but what about the couple? If they are to trust a minister they do not already know, they will want to see something of the person he is. Even when they are acquainted with him, they will need to have confidence in whatever he may invite them to do. They will need to have some sense of the role or roles he is performing.

In chapters 6, 7 and 8 three distinct, but overlapping, roles will be considered in terms of three separate tasks:

(a) reviewing the decision to marry, which is related to a counselling role (chapter 6);
(b) learning about marriage, which is related to a teaching and training role (chapter 7);
(c) celebrating marriage, which is related to the roles of being a minister of Church and gospel — a spiritual guide, celebrant and preacher (chapter 8).

In the final chapter more consideration will be given to the minister's sense of marriage and how he personally invests these roles with significance.

The habit of observation

Tape recordings have introduced many of us for the first time to the sound of our own voices; now video recordings can show us how we act. Their use in many forms of training has become common practice. In an opening interview much can be gained or lost because of the way a minister behaves and engages in conversation. We may need to learn how we deal with people and recognise the effect this has upon them by observing and attending to seemingly trivial details. The following examples have been chosen to illustrate some basic points. At this point in the book it might be useful to note down your own observations and comments as you work through the examples. If you are also in a position to record verbatim, or ask someone to observe, what you do in practice, that would be very useful. Not only what we say of course, but the way we say it and the gestures that accompany the words, need to be noted. If you are going to record live or ask someone to sit in when you are interviewing a couple, their consent will be needed and confidentiality preserved.

The task to be observed in the first interview is the building of a connection between the concerns of the minister and of both partners, and the establishing of a relationship between them in which everyone can be honest and communicate clearly with each other. It is not simply a matter of friendliness all round but of securing a working relationship in which the minister can be seen to have a clear and appropriate role with regard to the couple's reasons and needs for being there.

Suppose a minister is seeing a couple for the first time. The basic information needed (date, time and legal eligibility to marry) has been considered and is satisfactory. The minister now intends taking about half an hour to build up a degree of trust and rapport with the couple and to do so in a way that will encourage them to say what they want to each other, in front of him. This will lay a foundation for further conversation. Consider two questions:

- Are you enjoying making the arrangements for your wedding?
- Before you came tonight did you have any idea what I might ask you or say to you?

Can you foresee where they might lead in a conversation? Do you use questions like this yourself, or would you want to be more directive? How about this:

Getting married is a team effort. You and I, and your families all have parts to play and we need to know what each of us is supposed to do. You've made an effort to be here tonight and I'd like to encourage you to discuss what you need from me. It would be a pity if afterwards you realised there was something you meant to ask or say, and didn't. You can always come back to me, of course, but that takes time. First I'm going to ask you to tell each other about one thing we've done or spoken about already, that you expected. Secondly, tell each other what you want to talk about and which we haven't mentioned yet. Don't worry about speaking out in front of me; I wouldn't have asked you to do it if I thought you or I would be embarrassed.

Do you think this introduction is too condescending? Do you think couples will express surprise and even annoyance at being asked to 'play games' like this? Would you set about it differently?

Having begun to recognise some of the issues in a practical way, it may be helpful to look in more detail at how interviews can develop under different kinds of direction.

Example 1

In the first five minutes the minister has obtained details of the names, dates of birth, marital status, occupations and addresses of both partners. Together they have checked on the spelling of personal names and determined how old each partner will be on the wedding day. The partners' names are Bill and Susan. Bill is already living at the house they will both make their home in. The minister also needs for the marriage register details of their fathers' names and occupations. Because he does not know if both sets of parents are married or divorced, or whether the fathers are still alive, he asks the next question in a general way.

MINISTER: Are both your parents still alive and living at home?

BILL: Well my Mum lives at home with my younger brother and sister but my Dad's living away. My parents split up when I was nineteen.

(*pause*)

MINISTER: What did you feel about that when they split up — can you remember?

BILL: Well I didn't like it and my sister was really upset. She was only twelve and she didn't want our Dad to go. Me and my brother were upset but we didn't show it like she did. My mother didn't much either. I don't really understand what went on between them.

MINISTER: Does Susan know all that? It's part of your family story and I wonder if it's something you have talked about together.

SUSAN: I think Bill has talked to me a lot about it really because we met not long after his father went off.

BILL: Yes, I was glad to have someone outside the family to talk to and it wasn't something I could share with my friends. My close friends from school knew about it but I was a bit ashamed. I know it happens to people a lot nowadays, but you don't actually think of it happening to your parents.

MINISTER: Is it going to make it awkward for you both at the wedding?

SUSAN: I don't think so. My Mum and Dad know about Bill's parents and they like Bill. It could happen to anyone. Jane, that's Bill's sister, is going to be a bridesmaid. I think it's going to be a very happy day.

BILL: That's right. My Mum's looking forward to it. My Dad's going to come. He's living with someone else now but he's going to come on his own. I don't know whether he will sit with Mum—he doesn't have to does he?

MINISTER: No—it's up to your parents to decide that. You may have to raise the question with your Mum if she doesn't mention it . . . but that depends on how easy you find it to sort things out in your family. Some families talk a lot about things together; other families tend to get by, somehow avoiding difficult conversations.

BILL: We'll have to see; we don't talk a lot about things in our family. We're not like Susan's family.

MINISTER: Do you and your parents talk a lot together Susan?

SUSAN: Yes, I think we do. I've got an older brother and he is like my father a bit. They enjoy teasing my Mum and me. We have a lot of fun really. I like it when we get together with my Nan and my aunts and uncles too. Some of them live close and so we see a bit of them. They'll all be at the wedding too.

MINISTER: Bill, have you met many of Susan's family?

BILL: We've been to see her Nan—she's great. She's about seventy now, but real fun. We went to see her when we got engaged. None of my grand-parents are alive now—except my father's mother but we haven't seen her for years.

MINISTER: Susan, do you think that you and Bill have very different family backgrounds?

SUSAN: What do you mean? Are you saying we aren't suited to each other?

MINISTER: No, I am not saying that. What I mean is this— when two people get married they have in one sense to make a break with their parents and yet in another sense they take their family with them into their marriage. For example, if Bill learnt in his family to get by without sharing too much of his personal feelings and your family, Sue, was one in which you could talk about what you felt or at least show your feelings, you will each bring those different experiences to your marriage. The fact that they may be different experiences doesn't mean you aren't suited to each other. It may be one of the things that attracts you to each other—you balance each other. When you're living together as a married couple some of these different ways of behaving will become obvious to you—they may worry you or annoy you at times. It's helpful to recognise how much your behaviour has been learnt from your family. That's why I asked the question. It's important for you both to meet each other's family. I think you've done that. It's also important for you to start to share your life story with each other. Does that make sense?

SUSAN: Yes it does, though I think it's something you take for granted too.

MINISTER: Yes, indeed. What kind of things do you take for granted?

(*Pause*)

SUSAN: Well it's hard to say, just like that.

BILL: I think I know what you mean. Susan always hugs and kisses her family when she comes away, but we don't do that with mine—well we do but it's sort of quieter.

SUSAN: Yes, and at your house we usually go to the front door when we call, and if you haven't got a key we ring the bell, but at my house everyone goes round the back.

MINISTER: And what do you feel about that, does it make any difference?

SUSAN: Well I think it's important for people to be able to drop in and feel welcome. I always feel welcome when I go to Bill's house. I think his family are just a bit shy in some ways. That's nice too sometimes.

I like my noisy family but sometimes it gets a bit
on top of you. I used to get really cross with my
brother and father sometimes—they're kind, don't
get me wrong, but sometimes men go too far when
they are teasing you or having a joke. Bill is very
gentle and considerate.

MINISTER: Bill, what do you feel about what Susan has just
said?

BILL: I don't know really—I suppose I am different from
her father and brother and they are the two men
she has spent most of her life with so far.

Comment

The conversation becomes more intimate when Bill explains
about his parents. The minister follows this up by developing
some conversation about family background. His initial
response to Bill does not probe too far the possibly painful
experience of the parental break-up; but there is some
relevance in discussing Bill's reactions to his parents' marriage
and the extent to which he has shared them with Susan. The
question the minister has to consider is how far he should
probe at all and whether he should do so at this early stage.
What he does do is to respond to what Bill tells him. His
parents' separation is something Bill appears to be comfortable
talking about. The minister then checks whether the two of
them have talked about this before, and encourages Bill to
raise a practical question about seating the family at the
marriage service. The minister may in fact have been
sensitively anticipating an eventual question from Bill. He is
also showing that he is not embarrassed to talk about people's
divorces and that may help Bill and Susan to gauge how
understanding he is.

Having dealt a bit with Bill's family, the minister may be
looking for an opportunity to bring Susan's own family
experience into the discussion. Bill gives him a chance by
saying 'We're not like Susan's family'. He follows on by
asking Susan a difficult and analytical question. Her reply
may indicate that he is moving too fast and has aroused her
anxiety about what these questions are for. He attempts to

dispel that anxiety and explains his reason for posing the question. Bill shows he is prepared to try to answer the question. The two begin to share in an exploration of what they know of their family background and Bill provides encouragement for Susan to do this.

It is apparent that Bill and Susan are both intelligent and able to talk about themselves with some honesty. The minister is moving at a fast pace—a lot of information has been forthcoming. He is using the interview in order to develop and share personal knowledge based on experience. This suggests that he is introducing the couple to the kind of conversation that might provide them with the opportunity to learn more about themselves, and it may be one way of preparing the ground for further activity. He may wish to ask them to come to several more meetings, and in order to secure their agreement and commitment he has to give them some idea of what will be involved. He therefore chooses to use the first meeting to set out his approach and to begin to demonstrate how he would engage the couple in further conversation; it appears that he did that quite deliberately.

Some basic guidelines

If you have looked critically at this first illustration you may now recognise that certain actions are helpful in establishing rapport:

1. The minister is receptive to what both partners are saying and pays attention to the feelings and convictions expressed;
2. both partners are drawn into the conversation;
3. the minister does not question too hard or too quickly; he is careful not to put either partner under pressure;
4. the questions he asks require more than a yes/no answer;
5. the minister avoids lengthy monologues.

Doing this also means relying on intuition heightened by experience. If the minister has a plan in his mind, as the conversation develops he will be aware of how far it is going in the way that he expected. If he is to work with what a couple share of their own experience, the plan he uses will need to be flexible, and organised around topics or themes that are related to human experience, rather than abstractions.

Our first example fits a context in which a minister sees each couple getting married from their first enquiry through to the wedding ceremony, and might in some cases maintain contact with them afterwards. Through this sequence he may move from one role to another and will possibly continue to exercise one, while introducing another. He moves from being an official to being a kind of a teacher and possibly to acting as a counsellor. Were someone else to take the preliminary meeting, he would have to find another basis on which to begin working with the couple; to repeat questions they had already been asked might simply annoy them.

Example 2

In our second example, a minister is interviewing two people who are both under twenty. He decides to encourage them to think about whether they are ready to be married. Consider the following opening conversation and make a note of your observations. How would you rephrase what the minister says, in order to encourage a more positive response from the couple?

MINISTER: Well you are both very young. Do you think you are wise planning to get married this year?

INTENDING BRIDE: Yes, we want to get married now. We've been going out for a couple of years and we know we love each other, so what's the point of waiting?

INTENDING GROOM: If we wait it won't be any cheaper or easier to get somewhere to live. And two can live as cheaply as one, so we'll save money by getting married.

MINISTER: Well do you think you have a secure job? Do you think you can support your wife if you don't have secure prospects?

INTENDING GROOM: Well my Dad manages all right and he's on the dole. Anyway both of us are working at the moment.

MINISTER: Do you know that when people marry as young

as you are planning to, there is four times as much chance that they will end up getting divorced?

INTENDING BRIDE: But who says we're going to end up divorced? My Mum was only eighteen when she married and she and my Dad are still together.

INTENDING GROOM: Anyway, suppose we wait two years, we'll still be the same people getting married won't we, so being older or younger doesn't make any difference.

Comment

It sounds as if the minister isn't the first person who has had this conversation with this couple; they have their answers ready. The minister may have given the couple little room to discuss any doubts that they do have. They have been put on the defensive. If they have formed the impression that he is actually against them getting married, they may not recognise any genuine insights that he is able to share with them. This minister has begun on a negative note; is it not better to begin in a positive way by addressing the couple's perceptions of what they are doing?

Revised Example

Assuming that the minister has already taken time to break the ice, the conversation might proceed along these lines.

MINISTER: You know you are both old enough to get married. Have you thought about what it will mean to be married? What are some of the changes it will bring in your life? (*Pause*) For example what difference has going out together already made to you? (*Pause*) Mark, can you think back two years and compare how life was for you then, with how things are now? Can you suggest one difference that going steady with Karen has made to you?

MARK: I don't go round with my mates so much.

MINISTER: How much less do you see of them?

MARK: Well we used to meet up most nights and definitely at the weekends. Now I see them once a week, sometimes twice.

MINISTER: What other differences are there?

MARK: I feel more settled, responsible you could say.

MINISTER: Do you like that?

MARK: Well, Yes, and No.

MINISTER: Yes, and No. OK. Now Karen, you have a turn. What difference has going out with Mark made to you?

KAREN: The same. I just see my friends once a week now. And I don't spend so much money. I save more, saving to get married.

MINISTER: Is it worth saving to get married?

KAREN: It gives you a better start. Anyway I want to get married. I'd much rather be with Mark than hanging around with my friends or wondering who will take me out. I know when we do go out as a gang and do things together we have a good time, but it's all the better for being less often.

MINISTER: It sounds as if you like enjoying yourself, so what's one of the things that attracts you to Mark? Something you enjoy about being with him when you are out together?

KAREN: He's funny. He doesn't take things seriously. He likes a joke and a laugh. He cheers me up.

MINISTER: Mark, do you see yourself like that, not too serious?

MARK: Yes, I like making people laugh. There's enough serious people around without me adding to them, that's what I think.

MINISTER: You mentioned 'feeling more responsible' a moment

ago. I thought you had mixed feelings about being settled and responsible. What's the thing that you don't like so much? Is it the seriousness?

MARK: Yes, that's it really. I don't mind getting married and I want to marry Karen. I feel old enough, but I don't want it to get all serious. I don't want to get in a rut.

MINISTER: Do you and Karen talk about this sometimes?

Comment

There may be some way to go yet, but the conversation has broken through some of the barriers to honest discussion. By a gentle approach and by not putting Mark under immediate pressure, the minister has made it possible for Mark and Karen to recognise some feelings and convictions they have about getting married.

The minister was careful not to get into abstract ideas; a word like 'commitment' might just stop the conversation. Perhaps he is not yet sure how much Mark and Karen see things long-term. Karen is obviously aware of the wisdom of saving a bit to give her a start in marriage, but the goal is 'getting married'. It is not at all clear why Mark wants to get married, except that he knows that he is old enough to do so and likes Karen. Although he plays the joker, perhaps he is inwardly attracted to being responsible as well. Karen's trust in him could be evoking that need to be thought to be responsible. These are hunches that the minister may want to test out as the conversation develops. He will be careful not to let his own assumptions control the questions he is asking; the responses he gets from Mark and Karen will suggest the course to take.

One way of introducing the notion of commitment would be to develop conversation about the way that Mark and Karen are attached to one another: what kind of bond already exists between them and how has it developed? The experience of attachment lies at the heart of commitment. If both partners are willing, the minister may deliberately prompt a conversation about their experience of growing more attached to each other in order to recognise important moments as each of them sees it. Firstly they may recognise and tell each other about moments when each of them felt more deeply attached because of something that happened or was said. Was there an occasion when one of them was conscious of wanting to be faithful or loyal, of deciding to exclude relationships with other people or of making a deliberate choice? Was there an occasion when one of them consciously gave up something or someone for the sake of the other? Does the idea of giving up some personal freedom or ambition because of this attachment and love remind them of any time when they did something for, or thought about, the other? These are thoughts and perceptions the partners might share with each other and the minister's role is to guide them to do so while taking sensitive account of their own wish for privacy.

This is just one example. It is possible to imagine an interview with another couple proceeding quite differently. Yet focussing on actual experience is vital. Some partners may be much more inclined to use abstract ideas and the minister might feel very at home in such conversation, saying more and talking about the nature of marriage. By slipping into a discussion about generalisations, the minister may miss an opportunity. Words and ideas need to be related to couples' own experiences. Those who talk easily or who are able to intellectualise, may fail to give due account to their emotions and deep convictions.

Example 3

David is a priest who gives priority to offering couples a conscious preparation for their marriage ceremony. He believes that if he can establish a good working relationship with each couple and help them to take responsibility for their marriage service, he will have done what they need and what he is expected to do as a priest. He does not have a set pattern of pre-wedding interviews; he is prepared to give whatever time it takes and reckons that over a year in which he might take ten weddings, the time he spends with each couple averages out at about four hours.

When Louise and Robert come to see him about getting married their planned wedding day is nine months away. They are both nervous because they do not really know what is involved, although they have recently been to the wedding of some friends. David asks them what they remember about that wedding, prepared to make a few notes that will help later on when they talk about their service. He asks them to remember what they noticed and felt about that service, things they liked and things they disliked. He prompts Robert to start first. Robert remembers that the bridegroom had not seemed too flustered; he had said his words very clearly. He thought the vicar was very cheerful with everyone and did not say too much or waste time, which was a good thing because the church had been pretty cold. He did not remember much of the service; he had not known the hymns and when they came to the Lord's Prayer the words were different and not many people joined in. He liked the church; it was 'modern and you could see what was going on'.

Louise thought the service went well; it had been her friend who had been getting married. She liked the hymns and she remembered that some of the words in the vows had sounded different from what she thought they were. She had liked the service; it had made sense to her and it had not sounded old-fashioned. She is quite nervous about having to say her vows because she knows everyone will be listening to her. 'Does it matter if you get them wrong?' David answers that question straightaway by saying he has known many people to be nervous, but usually they have not made mistakes. Usually they are spoken line by line; that way they are not difficult to repeat. There would be more time nearer the wedding to talk about the vows and then have a rehearsal. David says it is his job to make sure that they both know what they have to do and he is there to guide them through it. What will help them when they say the words will be knowing that they want to marry one another.

At this stage he is content with the way the couple are responding. He thinks they may have expressed some of their thoughts about their own wedding through recalling what they felt about someone else's. David asks them if there is anything else they want to know about; he will do his best to answer their questions or help them to find the answers. He says he expects them to feel a bit uncertain about what they are doing and since they want everything to go well, it is worth asking now about anything that is bothering them. Louise asks whether she has to wear a veil, because she does not really want to, but her mother thinks she should. David says there is no rule about a veil and you do not have to wear one just because you are a bride coming to church. Perhaps Louise's mother feels very strongly about it because she got married in a veil and she thinks it is the right thing to do, but fashions change. He says that it is Louise's decision what she wears and she will probably be influenced by convention and her mother's ideas as well as by what she feels about the significance of wearing a veil.

David wondered how much to say at this stage in dealing with that question. He thinks he has already said more than enough, but he is aware that Louise's ability to resolve the decision satisfactorily may depend on her readiness to put her relationship with her mother on a different footing. Making her own decisions about her wedding is a way of adjusting to being a wife first and a daughter second. He decides that the issue to address is the question of who is arranging this wedding. How much do Louise and Robert need to plan and decide things together as a necessary part of identifying with the event? Clearly Louise's relations with her mother will also be an issue. David does not always consider it appropriate to open up a discussion about family relations but he recognises that they affect the wedding arrangements, and may be worth looking at now.

Who are the people involved at the moment in planning the wedding? David gets out a large sheet of paper. He gives Louise and Robert a marker pen each and asks them to write down the names of the people involved as they think of them. The names of those who are most closely involved could be written towards the centre of the sheet. He asks them to start with themselves: are they both equally involved? Robert puts himself off to the right; Louise is in the centre with her Mum close by. Robert adds his own mother and father close to his name. Louise has added her aunt who is making the cake and the people who will be catering for the reception. There is a pause so David draws a rough egg shape to enclose the names on the sheet, and asks if anyone else ought to be added inside the line because they too have something to do with the wedding. Louise thinks of her Dad because he has to give her away, though he does not seem very interested in things at the moment. And there are the bridesmaids who have been more or less chosen. Robert has not yet asked anyone to be best man.

There is another pause and so David takes another sheet of paper, draws the egg shape on it and asks Louise and Robert this time to write within it the names of people and their relative positions as they would prefer to see them involved in the wedding. Again he asks them to start with themselves. They pause so David asks whether they think they have an equal part to play. Louise says she would like Robert to be more involved. Robert says he is not sure what else he ought to be doing and he does not want to interfere with what Louise's Mum wants. His parents are being helpful to him in the background and they are helping him pay for his share of things. However as Louise's Dad is going to have to foot most of the bill he thinks it is only fair that her parents should have the main say. Louise says that does not matter, she still wants Robert to be involved, it is 'our wedding', she says, and not theirs.

David asks them again to try and draw the new arrangement as they would like people to be involved. Louise writes her name with Robert's in the centre of the page and then adds her Mum and Dad off to the left and Robert's parents off to the right. They add a few more names including some more members of both families. It is not clear whether they are just talking about the wedding service or whether they are talking about the whole celebration. David's name does not actually appear; did he expect them to add it? At this stage he does not comment on his own position; it is up to Louise and Robert to perceive that as they go along. He now suggests to Louise that whether or not she wears a veil is only part of the picture. How do she and Robert want to discuss things with their parents? How much do they want to involve them in the details? How much are they prepared to let their parents do things the way they want? He asks whether they have talked

enough about it for the moment; would they like to go away
and work things out a bit more together? They both agree.

David is already aware that Louise and Robert are
uncertain of their roles, that they are half wanting to be in
control and that they have ideas that they have not fully
discussed together. For their part, they are aware that this
wedding is something of a family occasion, and they want to
meet their families' wishes. The next time they come David
will need to check how plans have moved on but he will also
want to go on from the point they have reached this time, by
helping them both to recognise how they can make the
wedding their own rite.

Using the trust

These illustrations show how the three tasks and roles that
will be explored in chapters 6, 7 and 8 may emerge at a first
interview. Tasks that a couple may need to undertake but
which they do not necessarily embrace easily become apparent.
Each minister will have his own way of building the rapport
and indicating what task has to be done. Through understanding clearly the roles that are appropriate for him a
minister can extend the range of these tasks so that he can be
more flexible in the way he responds to each couple and more
resourceful in what he can offer them. The earlier he sees
them, the more scope he may have. A lot can be done before it
is appropriate to say, 'I'll get in touch with you nearer the
time'. The first of these important tasks may be easier to
tackle when two people are still learning what other people
think of their decision to get married.

SIX

Reviewing

'Are you trying to tell us we're making a big mistake, that we shouldn't be getting married?'

Being in love sounds like an essential pre-requisite for getting married until you ask yourself what it means to be 'in love'. Romantic love is presumed to be passionate, constantly fuelled by ardent longing. Its impetus is the very force which can break marriages as much as make them; an attraction that can be physical, sexual, needful or illusory. The view that romance is a basis for marriage was crisply countered by the writer Irma Kurtz in a television discussion in 1986 when she declared that instead of marrying the person you cannot live without, you should marry the person you can live with.[1] Living with someone in any way that is mutually fulfilling is likely to call for, and call forth, affection; it will also require compatibility. It is this blend of affection and realism that lies at the heart of a sensible decision to marry. Romance may provide an exciting prelude but to give a sure basis for an intended lifelong union there has to be love and reason.

How do you begin to encourage two people to review their decision to marry, to consider whether they are being sensible? Is this something they are likely to want, particularly at a time when they are concerned about preparing a wedding? Their attention is distracted. More than that, their minds seem to be made up; they behave as though the matter is closed. Clearly a person who intends to raise this basic issue will encounter resistance and has to have a legitimate reason for what he does. A minister has a moral and canonical duty to explain what marriage is so that couples may have no reasonable doubt as to what they are doing. Along with any explanation, he could offer them advice and invite them to consider carefully the reasons why they wish to marry. Many

59

ministers give couples books to read and consider privately
with that need in mind. This intention might be achieved in
an open and straightforward way by inviting each partner to
consider not only why they want to marry but what each will
be expressing to the other as they make their marriage vows.
A positive approach, inviting the partners to affirm what they
want to do, may overcome the first obstacle to conversation,
that is, the defence they mount to protect their sense of being
a couple already.

When a couple are presenting a united front in saying they
wish to be married, this is what we have to respond to. This
has to be the starting point for any sensible discussion.
Legally they are not yet married but socially at least they are
a couple and likely to defend their sense of being one against
anyone who tries to shake the foundations. The defence is
natural and necessary, for it is part of the business of
becoming the true couple they want to be. Part of the turmoil
of courtship is this struggle to displace other commitments
and loyalties in order to be together. (When two people living
away from home and established friends decide to get
married, this test may be delayed until they meet family and
old friends around the time of their wedding.)

The minister has to enable each partner to examine what
they are presenting as a sensible decision, without setting
himself over and against them. He starts by asking if they
would like to affirm this decision so that they can invest their
marriage ceremony with their own personal sense of what to
be married already means for each of them. They may believe
they know what each other thinks, and it may be the truth or
an illusion. The minister offers them a context in which they
can say it in front of him, in order to prepare to speak their
vows aloud before a congregation. He assists one or both of
them to do what they might not otherwise find very easy to
do: to articulate why they want to marry, what they hope for,
and what they are yet uncertain about. He will have to make
it safe for them. The method involves them sharing personal
matters with him; they will have to allow the minister to enter
their privacy and they will need to trust him with what they
disclose. It is important to know what self-disclosure does in
a relationship, so that a minister may understand the terms
on which he should work and what boundaries his role has.

Privacy, self-disclosure and intimacy

Privacy is the enclosure we create for ourselves in order to limit what others see of us. In times of tragedy or personal misfortune that defence may be unexpectedly breached; outsiders see what is happening to us as they catch sight of our deeper feelings. What people do at home, and in particular the details of their intimate relationships, are deemed to be private unless they choose to reveal them. Notice how reluctant even friends and relatives can be to interfere in marital matters. This is not a convention accepted in all cultures, particularly where marriages are made much more in the context of family kinship. As conventions vary, so the boundaries which provide privacy are differently drawn.

People will also regulate the boundaries they draw around themselves in order to control the degree of intimacy they want in particular relationships. A couple enraptured of each other may seek a lot of privacy in order to be more intimate; we might say they are totally wrapped up in each other. They remove part of the boundary between them as individuals in order to become more absorbed in each other. They risk dropping their guard to disclose their inner thoughts and feelings to each other. The process of self-disclosure if it is to be comfortable has to proceed at the pace both can accept, with each partner controlling what he or she shares, and both of them keeping this knowledge from others. When one partner is careless about this and breaks the trust by sharing some of this intimate knowledge with friends, the other may be hurt and angry.

This process of deepening intimacy can be seen in its effect on other relationships. A couple may demonstrate their closeness by giving each other a lot of attention, deliberately signalling they are a couple and holding other relationships at a distance. On the other hand they may be discrete about their affection when in other company, so as to evade enquiry or attention. This pattern of maintaining their identity as a couple and yet entering into other relationships as separate persons will be a recurring feature both before and after marriage and it can be a major cause of uncertainty and possible conflict. Many marriages are enriched by the way both spouses can enjoy close friendships with other people of

both sexes. Yet this possibility is often inhibited or marred by
the jealousy or anxiety of one of the partners. The signs that
this can occur are likely to be visible during the process of
becoming a couple. It cannot be assumed that two partners
have an equal desire to be intimate and it should be recognised
that many marriage partners sometimes wish to avoid
intimacy. To achieve the balance wanted, one partner may
regularly seek other company and at the same time reduce
the amount of privacy they can enjoy as a couple. Both
partners may collaborate to avoid being too much alone
together by engaging in a busy social life.

Intimacy has an obvious physical reference; closeness and
touching diminish bodily separation. A body is defined by its
skin and lovers explore this sensitive layer and bring their
bodies together as they play and cling to one another. A
woman may have to protect herself from a man until she is
ready to be known by him; her own readiness may depend on
her seeing that he too is ready for an intimacy that promises a
commitment to continuing closeness. A man may feel the
same about a woman. When a man or woman is looking for
sexual intercourse without emotional intimacy, he or she may
be reducing their capacity to form intimate and exclusive
relationships.

When partners deliberately hide much of themselves from
each other there can be an unreality about their being a
couple. One may set out to deceive the other and conceal
aspects of his or her character or past history which is
considered unattractive. As a result a partner may actually
know less about an intended spouse than that person's
established friends, a state of affairs that can create a dilemma
for other people who might wish to prevent an ill-considered
match. Yet they are likely to be held back by a belief that it is
not their business; the mantle of privacy has already begun to
filter not only what is conveyed by the couple but also what is
communicated to them. Somehow those who intend to marry
are expected to do their own finding out in courtship.

A minister who enters this privacy intending to encourage
the partners to talk to each other in his presence undermines
any conscious deceit. And even when a couple have already
been open with each other they may not wish to share that

knowledge in the presence of someone else. They need time to consent to such an interviewing process and they need to see the value it will have for them. Then they will need to control what they share and the pace at which they do so. They will be particularly wary of those matters on which they have doubts; they may worry that if something were known they would no longer be liked or attractive. On occasions it will be helpful to see partners individually, and certainly when one of them requests it. This might occur, for example, when a person has recently lost a previous spouse and wants to talk about his sense of guilt at marrying again.[2] Yet the substance of an individual interview may need to be shared with the other partner later, by mutual consent.

Any suggestion by the minister that both partners should have separate meetings with him, would be threatening to many couples even if it were reasonably explained. It might imply that he has something to say to one of them that he does not want the other to hear. If separate interviews are arranged both partners need to know that the minister expects them to share with each other whatever they want later. He still has to spend time with them both afterwards to follow up issues that needed talking about. Those who consider that separate interviews should take place as a matter of course, may believe this to be consistent with the particular counselling role they wish to adopt.[3] Yet to insist on this requires a different kind of contract with the couple from the one I am proposing here and it is one many couples would reject. On the other hand, a minister who is prepared to encourage separate interviews as and when he knows them to be necessary will need to act openly with the couple and demonstrate that he is responding to their cues as well as his own knowledge.

By focusing attention on a couple's decision to marry, the minister can offer a context in which the partners can begin to understand together what has been happening to them as individuals and as a couple. In counselling terms this first stage is the equivalent of taking a case history. But the issue is not so much a problem as a decision (at least until someone recognises that there is a problem). How did the decision to get married come about and what does it signify for each partner? To answer it requires some knowledge of where they have come from and what has happened to them in courtship.

Courtship Today

In this country courtship has conventionally provided one way in which men and women choose their marriage partners. Nearly 400 years ago John Dod recommended that 'he therefore which will know all his wife's qualities; or she that will perceive her husband's dispositions, and inclination, before either be married to the other, had need to see one the other eating and walking, working, and playing, talking, and laughing, and chiding too.'[4] Courtship properly gives time for the sentiment of love to mature and be enjoyed with a stable and continuing union in view. Two functions have to be balanced: maintaining sufficient emotional enthusiasm for getting married and learning enough to know that the choice of mate is a good one. Over the centuries courtship in England, apart from the wealthy classes, has commonly been initiated by the partners themselves lasting between six months and two years. Young men and women have generally been allowed to spend time together unchaperoned, a relaxed attitude that has often surprised foreign visitors but is important if the partners are to acquire familiarity with one another.

Many time-honoured procedures seemed still to be in evidence forty years ago when Geoffrey Gorer conducted a survey through *The People* newspaper.[5] He found little evidence of the whirlwind romance or of playing around before finding Miss or Mr Right; there was also little sign of the in-group marriage of old acquaintances characteristic of some settled communities. He found a difference between the working man from the north, who might marry the first girl he was seriously attracted to, and the middle-class girl from the south, who might consider several partners before allowing herself to become seriously attached. Two-thirds of the married men and half the married women who answered Geoffrey Gorer's questions claimed they had never seriously considered marrying anyone else. What the men most valued in their wives was the possession of the appropriate feminine skills and what the women most valued in their husbands was an agreeable character.

How far the situation has changed since then is not easy to gauge and personal observations and local experience may be more useful than any generalisations. The beginning of a courtship may now be less obvious and without clear, conventionally controlled, stages. More recent evidence comes from a study undertaken by Penny Mansfield and colleagues at the Marriage Research Centre.[6] Sixty-five couples who married (the first time for both partners) in 1979 in churches in London were interviewed three to four months after their wedding. Two-thirds of these brides and grooms had previously had serious relationships, in the course of which over half of them had considered marriage. The reason mostly given for ending those relationships was 'drifting apart'.

When looking at the course of the courtship that had led to their marriage the majority of couples interviewed considered they had at some point become engaged, some quite soon in their courtship and others only when they were clearly on course for getting married. Those who became engaged early were signifying that they were a couple although no wedding plans were made, and that sexual activity with anyone else was ruled out. Six couples had experienced interrupted courtships, meandering relationships which were broken off as many as four times, because one or both partners was not sufficiently ready to be married. Partners did not always make up their minds about marrying each other at the same time; one might come round to that way of thinking a month or even much longer after the other. About one in five of these newly-weds were consciously intent on being married, most of these 'marriage seekers' (but not all) being women. In these cases it was they who maintained the momentum towards marriage though their partners were apparently content to be led.

Most of the women started to date their eventual husbands in their late teens; the men would typically be two years older than the women. Sexual intercourse usually became a normal part of their courtship. The partners said they felt it was important to test sexual compatibility; either you were or you were not suited. Just over a quarter of the couples had lived together before marriage but the majority in the study did not favour this, mainly because of parental disapproval. Over three-quarters of those living together only did so when they had become committed to marriage and even then many of them had obscured the fact from their parents.

This study provides snapshot views of people's motives for marrying as they were understood at the time of the interview. The decision to marry seemed in many cases like a decision to stop being single. There was an inevitability about getting married though most found they did so younger than the ideal age at which they had once thought they would. Marriage, as well as being normal, was seen to provide adult status, the opportunity to have a place of your own, privacy and freedom to be yourself. Generally the partners in this study only began to think of marrying the person they were courting when they had become disposed to the idea of being married, but for as many as two-fifths of them significant events or outside circumstances seemed to have triggered the actual process in a significant way. A parent's remarriage, a serious illness, or the traumatic ending of one relationship, were examples. In some cases the departure of one partner on holiday or to another place coincided with a deepening of commitment on the part of one who had until then been hesitant. Yet the partners did not usually attribute great importance to these 'marriage triggers' when viewing the development of their relationship. Perhaps two people wanting to marry need to believe that they are in charge of the process and not subject to outside events.

Each couple's story

In a counselling relationship a couple's sense of being in charge of events can be enhanced by encouraging them to tell the story of their courtship in a way that helps them to take possession of certain knowledge, that is how they have grown together and how each has thought and felt about the other during this time. They come to recognise those habits of behaviour that have become established in the repertoire of their relationship, ways of treating and responding to each other, and private jokes bound up with memorable occasions.

They may not wish to talk about all this in front of someone else, but what they do and say then may encourage them to construct more of the story when they are alone together. The minister can provide them with a method for doing this in the way he asks them questions and comments on what they say. He may also demonstrate a way of seeing how their relationship has developed and changed in time, and how it carries the possibility of developing and changing further. Some couples may be helped if they see this drawn in some way; the simplest technique is to sketch a time line on a large sheet of newsprint using felt pens.

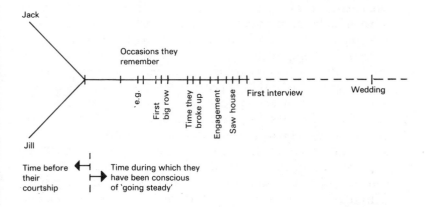

The first thing to establish on this time line is the date when the couple think they went out together or made a date for the first time. This occasion may not be clear, particularly if they were in a crowd and not consciously courting. One may recall the event with more certainty than the other. One of them may have continued to go out with other partners after this date. A lot of useful clues may emerge about their early interest in one another simply from trying to fix this date. They may have been acquaintances or even friends before that. How did this first date come about? Was it accidental or planned? Was it followed by a second date or did some time then elapse? At this early stage was one of them clearly taking a leading role? Establishing this date is a way of discovering the early dynamics of their relationship. What

pattern of meetings or encounters flowed from it and how
were they sustained? How was this different from any
previous experience of going out with other partners?

At this point in the story it may be relevant to look back
into the time before they consciously began courting. In
making comparisons, both partners may be inclined to play
down the significance of earlier relationships, but some
indication of how many other partners they have had and
how seriously they felt about them at the time, will help them
see the present relationship in perspective. The minister has
to guard against reading too much into these clues and it is
not his function to make deductions about the stability of
each partner. He is simply reminding them that they each
have an individual story from the time before they met which
may have had quite a bearing on their pathway to marriage.
A sense of being ready to settle down, of wanting a steady
and secure relationship, or of no longer enjoying casual
encounters, may be things people are willing to speak about.

It is likely that perceptions will be easier to share if they
somehow affirm the present relationship. Good times will be
easier to talk about, and the minister may have to make it
safe to talk about some of the bad times so that both partners
can look at them too. In doing this the minister is also
conveying to the couple that occasions when they may have
felt anger or diminished affection, or had a row, all provide
experience they can learn from. The simple message 'we
have to work through the difficulties to come to the joys' will
be more effectively conveyed by helping the partners attend
to some of those difficulties.[7] Through recognising different
events which have a watershed feel about them or which
represent a further milestone on the way, partners will become
conscious of how their commitment to each other has been
deepened. Such occasions as 'the time when I thought you
were going to move away', or 'the evening you didn't telephone
me after the match' are the notches on the time line that may
be worth marking because they recall thresholds of deepening
commitment and exclusivity. It is here that the conscious
wish to be married may become evident and related to
encounters with parents and families, the first meeting with
the minister and the process of preparing the wedding. How

is the relationship changing now as a result of all this? What convictions are being realised and what tensions are evident?

Generally speaking there are certain phases in this process of growing into being a couple. Firstly there is the time of recognition that 'this is the one for me'. This is an individual recognition, not necessarily reached together. When two partners can both confidently make that declaration to one another, a second phase has been reached. This mutual knowledge may still be very private, something to be guarded and nourished with intense repetition. The third phase is apparent in the activity of going public about this commitment. The recognition of these phases is important for understanding the significance of the marriage ceremony. In law the marriage begins with the ceremony but in the minds and hearts of the partners it begins somewhere between this second and third phase, when they know themselves that they want to be married. Yet that marriage cannot be properly established until the significant people in their individual stories have overtly consented to their marriage by witnessing it or acknowledging it.

Sexual experiment, lasting union

Part of the story a couple may wish to keep private, mostly from the minister, but partly too, perhaps, from one another is the physical sexual dimension. During the last two decades, young people appear to have been increasingly casting caution aside in the pursuit of excitement and freedom, even allowing that those who have caught the limelight may be the more confident and assertive of their generation. Oral contraception has provided a means for a majority of them to experience sexual intercourse without practical constraint before marriage. It is not clear if the fear of Aids will greatly alter that trend, especially among those involved in more than casual relationships. The messages delivered through the popular media and strengthened by peer group influence have fostered the notion that to hold back shows that one lacks passion; to be without a sexual partner can be interpreted, albeit unreasonably, as a sign of abnormality. A parallel notion has also

taken hold of many people's minds: if you are good in bed
together, then you are compatible.

In a sexual relationship two people may see the stage at
which they have physical intercourse for the first time as an
indication of how 'serious' they are. In general terms, there
are three obvious groupings. There are those who do it almost
the first time they go out together. Secondly there are those
pairs for whom sexual intercourse is linked to their sense of
being a couple. Then there are those who marry first and
make love together for the first time after that. In the first
group you might expect to find men and women who are
more likely to regard physical intercourse as an action distinct
from love and affection in a committed relationship. In the
second group you might find some partners who have found
that intercourse caused them to feel they were now a couple
as well as those for whom intercourse was an expression of
their knowledge that they were a couple. The third group
might include some who have yet to feel emotionally ready as
individuals as well as those who have chosen to wait until
they were married.

The sense of being a couple is largely subjective, while
getting married is much more clearly objective. Neither sense
nor ceremony necessarily guarantees the permanence of the
relationship, even though marriage carries that expectation
by law and it is still probably the understanding of the
majority. Those who have become accustomed to casual
sexual relations may consider they have just been shopping
around, but they cannot reasonably be confident that they
will change their habits when they find someone to whom
they feel deep commitment. If they are now intending a
permanent relationship it may be important for them to come
to terms with their behaviour so far. Some men and women
discover more deeply than others that sexual intercourse has
begun to bind them to their partner; yet it is not the first act
alone but the regular and comfortable renewal of it over time
that establishes the personal bond underlying the permanency
of marriage. Each partner will experience the strength and
depth of that bond differently.

Many men and women choose to be monogamous; for them
sexual intercourse cannot be detached from a faithful bond

which is exclusively with one person. Marriage is a recognised lawful way of making that a moral bond of lifelong intention. A couple who make love together before they marry are also demonstrating something of their attitude to the meaning and status of the law of marriage by saying that they do not have to be married to make love. One or other may not be agreeing to more than serial monogamy, in other words faithfulness to one partner at a time.

As in marriage, so before marriage, great anguish can be caused when there is such an imbalance in the level of commitment between the partners that one wishes to end the relationship and the other does not. Those who have made love before marriage may find as many moral and emotional obstacles to separating as do those who are married and have legal constraints to recognise as well. In fact because the status of a sexual relationship outside marriage is objectively unclear, partners may find it harder to resolve a potential rift than if they had been obliged to pursue a legal process to achieve a separation.

A continuing sexual union outside marriage needs mutual agreement and reciprocity of feeling to maintain it, but such a union established by lawful marriage has a certain external strength given to it so that it can be sustained for a time when the commitment is unequal, as it often may be. The process through which people have come to marriage in the last twenty years has been increasingly affected by a muddle of influences and overturned convention. Many adults have become better equipped to talk about sexuality and relationships, feelings and attitudes, with less repression and hypocrisy, but some of the valuable mechanisms implicit in careful courtship may now need to be retrieved.

Putting the families in the picture

When two people have decided to get married, their families are usually soon caught up in the process. Indeed there is a delayed effect if they are not. A couple who get married without the involvement of their families may have inadvertently or deliberately missed out some of the stages of courtship. Seeing partners in relation to the significant people in their lives will not only provide clues to hidden features of their personality; it may also illuminate aspects of a couple's own interaction. Early relationships play a significant part: fathers and mothers are role models in marriage, as well as people who may have profoundly affected a person's capacity to love and share intimacy. Deep affection for brothers and sisters may be the standard against which a relationship with anyone else is measured, and these affections may not be displaced by marriage. By encouraging partners to see each of these significant members of their family in their relative positions and to signify the kind of relationship they have with them, a minister will be ensuring that this essential family dimension to a marriage is not disregarded. One way of doing this is to supplement the time line with a two-generational or three-generational family tree, or genogram,[8] in which the status of those who are specially close or important is highlighted. Another method is for each partner to imagine their wedding photograph depicting those who will probably be present, together with those each partner wishes could be present. Attention to the family presence at a wedding and in marriage is a recurring theme throughout this ministry.

Pre-marital assessment

Another way of providing a couple with knowledge about themselves that they may choose to use in the process of getting married is to work with an inventory or questionnaire. In Canada and the United States ministers and counsellors are beginning to make use of quite sophisticated pre-marital inventories which can be analysed by computer. When the results have been obtained the minister and couple meet to interpret the results and talk about areas of the relationship the partners wish to look at and try to enhance.[9] Once again the value of such techniques is that they provide information that the couple can use for their own good. Inventories have to be carefully devised and be acceptable to those who are asked to complete them. Many partners would resent being asked repetitive and apparently banal questions, in order to learn about their relationship. Their appeal for some users will lie in their apparent objectivity; the couple are not subjected to the minister's whims and assumptions but gain their insight from an external and unbiased source.

Wherever the insights come from, in the end it is the partners themselves who decide to get married and they have to reverse the decision if they think it a bad one. Whatever the strength of his perceptions, the minister is powerless to prevent a bad match. The effectiveness of any review of the decision to marry will depend on the extent to which it engages the couple and gives them the means to change their minds if that is necessary. But for most couples its main value will be the light it sheds on some of the dynamics of their own relationship, and the impetus it gives them to learn together.

Notes

1. *Choices*, BBC 1, 20 July 1986.
2. A few issues like this are dealt with in Appendix B.
3. See, for example, the approach advocated by Mitman, J., in *Premarital Counselling*, New York: Seabury 1980, p. 23.
4. Dod, J., and Clever, R., *A Godlie Forme of Household Government*, quoted in Macfarlane, A., *Marriage and Love in England 1300—1840*, Blackwell 1986.
5. Described in Gorer, G., *Exploring the English Character*, quoted by Marwick, A., in *British Society since 1945*, Pelican 1982. For a Welsh perspective see also Leonard, D., *Sex and Generation*, Tavistock 1980.
6. A brief outline is given in Mansfield, P., *Young People and Marriage*, Occasional Paper no. 1, Scottish Marriage Guidance Council 1985. For a more detailed account see the same author's *The Beginning of the Rest of Your Life?* (with Collard, J.), Macmillan 1988.
7. Some suggested ways of exploring these experiences are given in Appendix B.
8. Stahmann, R. F., and Hiebert, W. J., *Premarital Counselling*, Lexington, MA: Lexington Books 1987, describe the use of this method for exploring family of origin with great clarity and detail; genograms are also described in Walrond-Skinner, S., *Family Matters: The Pastoral Care of Personal Relationships*, SPCK 1988, and in Purnell, D., *Exploring Your Family Story*, Melbourne: Joint Board of Christian Education 1983.
9. Some examples are described in Stahmann and Hiebert, op. cit.

SEVEN

Learning

'You don't really know about marriage until you're married yourself.'

Two people will not know clearly in advance what *their* marriage is going to be like, but they might already have seen a good deal of how marriages work and how married people behave. Their marriage will be shaped by the attitudes and ways of behaving that they have already developed before they marry, as well as by those unknown events and circumstances that will attend their life together. Much is still to come: that is their mystery. There is plenty to learn from in the present without trying to anticipate the future. In fact there is a natural inertia in many people against preparing for things in advance, as well as a resistance to change.

Learning about marriage, without being a deliberate activity, is hard to separate out from the lifelong process through which people grow and change. In the first years of a person's life a great deal of experience is retained in the unconscious; then and later it strongly affects people's feelings about themselves, their sexuality and the way they relate to others. As they grow up children may observe and learn from the ways their parents and other members of their household and their circle of acquaintances behave. When two people marry this experience is brought together and will at times give rise to conflict. Yet the breadth and variety of that experience can also be a great asset in a marriage, enabling a couple to respond to events and needs which might be puzzling or daunting to them as individuals.

As two people become a couple, they may be glad to say, 'all that I am I give to you, and all that I have, I share with you'. And they may become aware of how this includes the knowledge they bring to each other: a sense of the past within

74

them known in the present. Some of the discoveries made can provoke anxiety and the unfolding of them will be cautious as well as compelling. In reviewing how they decided to be married by presenting their story of becoming a couple they were looking at what they knew of each other through their experience in courtship. It may now be possible to build on that by looking more directly at their feelings, attitudes and ways of behaving. The following quotation refers to learning about parenthood but can appropriately be applied to the way people are prepared to be partners in marriage.

It is not feasible, even if it were desirable, to chart the course which couples might take in becoming parents since the passage can be made in so many different ways. Nor is the problem simply one of catering for a diversity of circumstances, the expectations we have about the future, our tendency to look on either the bright or gloomy side of life, our degree of resistance to change and preference to go it alone, for example stem from emotional conviction born of life experience. They reflect learned ways of coping with uncertainty which may or may not facilitate adaptation, but which go some way to define us as people. Programmes designed to promote educational health in the family are likely to be approached with caution because they might challenge cherished assumptions which we hold about ourselves and our world. . . . I would say that different experiences of parenthood have to be lived to be discovered and cannot effectively be learned about in advance. The pressing need is to provide conditions in which people can acknowledge their experience, good and bad.[1]

That statement points to the natural task, acknowledging and learning through experience; and points out the central obstacle, people's natural resistance to change within themselves. It is clear yet again that a person has to consent willingly to take part. People cannot be compelled to learn and any suggestion, for example, that you have to 'come on our course' to be married 'in our church' is quite likely to provoke resistance. Couples will more probably agree to come along if they have begun to see for themselves that there are things they can learn about now, that will help them to secure their marriage. They will probably be more willing to take part in a course or series of interviews if they think they will enjoy themselves, be treated as sensible people, and not be made to feel uncomfortable in the process.

The Churches have had the credit for pioneering educational work with couples getting married[2] and there has been a trend away from instruction towards informal discussion. Over the years churches have arranged courses for those getting married and here there has been a shift away from large gatherings at which couples are addressed by experts on such matters as finance, housing, the law and the physical facts of sex, towards meetings of small groups of couples led by one or two people with an ability in counselling or group work. The experience of marriage guidance counsellors has often been valuable in planning and leading these activities.[3] There is now a growing emphasis on encouraging partners to look at their expectations of married life, and on fostering helpful ways of communicating, expressing affection and handling rows. This is a move towards a person- or couple-centred approach, both conjointly and in group activity which is illustrated in the following example.

Example: an evening session with a group of couples

Margaret and Alan are two of a team of leaders used to conducting short workshops for engaged couples. The team they belong to is ecumenical, supported by several churches, and the priests and ministers involved have become confident about encouraging couples to take part in the three-session courses offered. Every six months the leaders and all the ministers meet together for a day to discuss and evaluate the courses, while routine decisions are handled by a director and small executive, all elected. The team includes several married couples, married people without their partners, a few single people and one who has been married and divorced. Margaret and Alan are both married but not to each other. (The team took a policy decision that married couples would not usually work together and that working partnerships within the team would normally change every year.) Margaret and Alan have previously led one course together and are now embarking on their second. There are four couples present for the first session, lasting two and a half hours.

The group has just finished an ice-breaking activity which included introductions. After a short break for tea and coffee there is an hour and a quarter in hand. Each couple are sitting together, and it is already apparent that two couples are getting on well together: the two women in the partnerships are sitting next to each other. Margaret begins to introduce the activity, aware that the other two couples are keeping to themselves. She asks each couple to move slightly apart so that partners can talk together, without easily overhearing what others will be saying. Then the two leaders give a picture to one partner in each couple, asking them to look at it silently.

One of three pictures is used (two copies of each are available). They show:

(i) a man and a woman standing embracing each other, the woman's hands encircle the man's head, they are looking at each other and the man is talking;

(ii) a man and woman separated across a table, there is no eye contact, the woman is sideways on to the man, busy cooking while she is talking and the man is sitting with his elbows on the table looking at her;

(iii) a man and a woman sitting together, bodies just touching, on a bench, neither saying anything to the other, both watching a young child feeding some birds.

After a pause Margaret asks the partner in each couple who is holding the picture to describe to the other what he or she sees in the picture. When they have done that the other partner is asked to suggest what may have been happening or could be about to happen to the couple portrayed.

Each leader now works with two of the couples and circulates the set of pictures ensuring that each couple spend five minutes studying and discussing each picture, each partner taking a turn at giving the description. Extending the fifteen minutes needed, Alan and Margaret take the opportunity at some point to engage each couple in conversation and encourage them to recall particular occasions when they have found themselves in one of those situations; each thinks of one memorable occasion and then tells the other what it was.

There is a buzz of conversation during which Margaret and Alan move a television and video recorder into position. The group repositions itself so that everyone can see the screen. (One couple sit on the floor for this.) Margaret briefly explains that she will show a film recording made up of two short extracts she has recorded from longer films and programmes, which show couples having some kind of conversation. The first extract lasts for five minutes. She asks each person to concentrate on what they see and hear going on. The extract shows a man and woman who turn out to be a married couple, remonstrating with each other, but showing a great deal of affection and humour in the process. When the extract has been seen Margaret introduces discussion by asking someone if they can put themselves in the shoes of one of the partners in the film and say what that person was feeling and trying to express. One of the women volunteers to talk about the woman in the extract and starts off; after a minute her partner interrupts her, taking the man's point of view. Alan intervenes quickly and asks the partner to hold off for a bit so that everyone can listen to another woman's point of view first. Someone else volunteers and carries on the conversation. When she has spoken, Margaret asks the male partner who had earlier interrupted to identify what the man in the extract was feeling and trying to express. When he has spoken for a few minutes, she asks if another man will offer another point of view about what the man might have been expressing.

After this some discussion develops across the group with participants beginning to comment on what other people have said. Alan asks if any of the men would like to suggest how the man in the film might have behaved differently towards the woman, perhaps positioning himself differently, speaking in a different way or touching her in some way. There is a pause and then one of the women asks if she can answer; she thinks that if the man had not walked around the room so much, but sat next to his wife instead, she would have been more inclined to listen to him. Alan draws out her ideas by asking one or two questions then allows other members of the group to comment before handing over to

Margaret to introduce the second film extract. This time Margaret explains that after watching it, each couple will be asked to discuss the extract on their own, and suggests that the men try to identify the feelings the woman in the film is trying to express, and vice versa. With thirty minutes in hand, she wants to leave time for some further conversation between partners before the session ends, so that she and Alan can again spend some time working with each couple to consolidate this simple exercise.

That example demonstrates a number of details about the way such groups can be led:

1. Initially two couples are still on their own in relation to the group as a whole. By asking each couple to find their own space to work in, Margaret provides a structure which removes any differentiation;

2. The leaders did not continue to control the first exercise formally but by circulating to join each couple encouraged them informally to keep to the task;

3. The leaders did not conclude the first exercise by offering an interpretation;

4. The change of seating arrangements to watch the video made it easy for couples to sit together but also focused attention away from themselves;

5. It was necessary to establish a few ground rules for the second exercise if individuals were to risk joining in. Alan's intervention supported Margaret's authority and discouraged interaction between the partners at that point. But Margaret soon responded positively to the man who had spoken;

6. It was possible in this exercise to use the anonymity of the film extract to enable people to speak out of their own experience without having to say they were doing so. The leaders were working together; their modelling could have given encouragement to the group to do the same and it was also a model of couple co-operation;

7. The final exercise made a deliberate return to working in couples. It might have been useful to stay longer working as a

group using the second film extract. It takes time to build up group cohesion and it would easily be lost between sessions. This had to be weighed against the value of encouraging partners to take up some of the issues together and recognise the way they communicate.

This example suggests that it may be an advantage to arrange for groupwork and raises a question about when it might be practicable.

Conjoint work or groupwork?

When both partners say they are willing to take part in some form of organised pre-marriage education is it better to see them simply as a couple together (that is, conjointly) or to invite them to join other couples?

Conjoint work is more likely to fit couples' expectations of pre-wedding interviews and it will be easier to arrange times and places where couple and minister can meet. There will be more opportunity to attend to each partner individually and to them both as a couple, and to respond directly to their actual behaviour and expressed feelings. In the presence of others they may be more wary of what they say and do, and how much they disclose. There will be those who are quite unused to talking about themselves in a group. Conjoint work can be undertaken by one minister alone and is likely to be an easier practical option, particularly where co-leadership might be difficult to provide.

Conjoint work will be unsatisfactory if a minister misuses any authority he has by encouraging or compelling partners to disclose more than they would otherwise agree to. An interview may become too intense for the couple's good; they may be disarmed by the intimacy of it and later regret what they were led to say or do. While it may be best for some couples not to take part in group activity, for many it might provide a better context for learning (as distinct from counselling). Couples may enjoy meeting others who are 'in the same boat' and they may be pleased to discover that the issues and adjustments they are facing are being experienced by others. One may be impelled to recognise one's own feelings when someone else is expressing similar ones:

likewise, by observing someone else's behaviour one can be made more aware of one's own, along with its effect on others. The peer group effect may encourage the confidence to say and do certain things which would be harder in the more intimate setting of conjoint work with one's partner. But all this depends on how far the group setting is trustworthy and people's perceptions of this will be affected by what they sniff out.

For many couples this kind of pre-marriage group may provide a valuable introduction to the possibilities of marriage enrichment later on. If the experience is a good one, they may see the point in later years of joining in a group or workshop for couples to explore and adjust to changes in their married life. Couples who have been involved in groups have often been glad to come to a reunion some time after their wedding — about six months to a year later often fits in well. It can be the first step in a follow-up series of sessions in which couples can benefit from their early experience of marriage at a time when many of them will only just be coming to terms with being married. It has been shown that educational activity by couples after they are married is much more effective than work beforehand.[4] But given that the wedding is the occasion that the Church has to respond to, attractive and constructive pre-marriage education is the most obvious way of generating the interest and potential.

The minister will have to consider the options in the light of what he knows to be practicable as well as preferable. If both approaches can be offered someone will have to be responsible for a screening process; not all couples will be suited to groupwork and not all will want it. It will mean some continuing provision for conjoint work even where group sessions are arranged.

Design

Between the totally unplanned 'see where we get to' approach and the finely detailed preplanned programme of sessions, there is a wide middle ground. Some deliberate design is needed if a couple as well as the minister are to have any idea of what is going on. Other people's schemes may be helpful but the design behind what a minister offers to couples has to be a personal one, a synthesis of what he knows he can do and what he has learnt that couples value. In theory the curriculum is wideranging; it is possible to detail a long list of potentially relevant aims, as might be discovered by using the exercise in Appendix A. Among the obvious topics would be communication, giving and receiving affection, recognising feelings, sexuality, gender and roles, parenting, values and priorities, conflict and decision-making. Ways in which some of these topics could be approached are suggested in Appendix B.

If partners have already undertaken some review of their decision to marry, in the way suggested in chapter 6, relevant topics or matters needing attention will be evident. There can be a valuable progression from review to learning. One author has suggested a three-phase programme linking the two.[5] He estimates that to be effective it would need to take approximately six to eight weeks and begin a year before marriage. The first phase would aim to increase couples' awareness of relationship strengths and potential problem areas and facilitate discussion of their relationship (linked to provision for counselling if serious problems need to be dealt with). The second phase would provide for discussion with other couples in small groups to increase their ability and willingness to share with others, develop friendships and learn how other couples relate and deal with issues. The third phase would use these small groups as a setting for skills training: communication skills like sympathy, empathy and self-disclosure, and skills for resolving conflict and problems. This phase would be more effective if it were delayed until six months after marriage. Such a design combines the merits of conjoint work, which meets individual needs flexibly, with group work designed to meet a range of needs forming some common ground.

Sequencing

This is a vital factor in design. Where people are reflecting on their own experience while interacting with others, one realisation may lead to another. What they discover by this method cannot be planned in advance but exchanges between people that may encourage it can be provided for. Prompts which help two people draw one another out in a listening exercise can be thought of in advance and adapted on the spot. In helping people to develop ways of resolving arguments, a simple technique of giving time to each other and listening can be tried and then improved upon in a subsequent activity. A sequence that makes sense helps people take initiatives and be more involved; participants are then more likely to come away knowing something they have learnt for themselves. When a minister has to keep on making links that participants have not begun to see for themselves, the process by which people can pursue their own learning is retarded. In conjoint work when the progression is unobtrusive and does not need pointing out too much, participants may become more relaxed and caught up in the process. (For example, a minister first makes use of some simple technique to improve communication and later asks the couple to use it in the course of discussing an issue between them that has arisen naturally.) In group work it is often necessary to outline the structure of sessions to engage people in activity and the thread can easily be lost if progress becomes too fast or too slow for some of those involved. Here the activities may have to be self-contained, with greater reliance on interaction to stimulate people's involvement.

There is a link to be sought between 'learning that' and 'learning how'. Partners' satisfactions with each other depend on each not only knowing what the other thinks or feels but also responding clearly and appropriately. It may, for example, be difficult for two partners who are very articulate to recognise the affective aspects of communication. Being in a group with people they might not have chosen to spend time with, may give them an opportunity to observe and value the way in which another couple say what they are feeling and respond to each other's moods. And the group activity may give them room to experiment and discover that they can be more affective in their behaviour. In a way the group allows people to go back to childhood and play, and do what children do naturally: learn by copying others. Thus an exchange of skills can arise naturally through the way individuals and couples begin to respond to one another. The leader can encourage it in the way he plans to use particular activities, makes use of a variety of resources and provides safe boundaries for the various interactions. A person may resist being told something by his partner but be willing to learn it from another person in the group. In conjoint work the minister will be working without this resource and may need to provide the model himself.

Feedback

The best way of ensuring realism is to plan into any programme of work simple ways of getting feedback. It provides evidence of what participants are thinking and feeling, but using it means being flexible. In a simple interview this may mean not attempting too much at a time, encouraging conversation between the partners early on, noticing how they behave and asking questions in order to find out something. Long sessions will rarely find the minister well prepared to respond effectively to all of the issues that arise, and concentrating on giving a long talk may leave little attention to pick up reaction. Feedback can be valuable for future planning; couples who take part in any courses or arranged series of meetings can be asked for their reactions. When they have had a few weeks to reflect on what took place, useful information can be gauged by asking them what they found useful, what in particular they think they gained, and what was not helpful. When these reactions and the minister's own notes of what happened are put with the observations of others who may be helping to lead or who are engaged in similar work, it is possible to make a quite useful evaluation. Some clergy and course leaders have also sought the reactions of couples after a much longer period of time.[6] Reactions then may be more critical, and express something of what, with hindsight, couples wish they had learned or had known about. Whether they would have accepted it at the time is another matter. Feedback from couples who have taken part could be combined in some cases with an invitation to help plan further activity and possibly assist in leading it. This approach has proved fruitful in a number of places.

When planning to use certain activities, prompt sheets or questionnaires, our first hand experience of trying to complete them ourselves before we use them with others is useful. Many training courses for leaders make deliberate use of the materials that might be employed in a course of sessions for others. This is a valuable opportunity to experience using different resource material and to recognise the feelings it can evoke and the memories that can be stirred. It is essential at the same time to learn from other people's reactions by providing for immediate feedback. It is also valuable to see the way another person introduces and directs activity; there are often several ways of using the same material.

This kind of training may be a sufficient introduction where leaders have some previous experience of learning in a group, will be leading with someone else and will have regular meetings to assess what has happened. Working with another person who already has some experience is good practice; couples who would like to work together are well encouraged to work with someone else first. When they do lead activities together they will find their own relationship affected by this work. Although it is not their task to present their own marriage as an example to be copied, the way they behave towards each other will act as a model for others, provoking conscious and unconscious reactions. Any areas in their own relationship that they have not been willing to address can constitute a no-go area that others will be able to sense. This observation should not be taken out of context; it applies here to this occasional ministry using groups led by volunteers. There are other kinds of activity structured in such a way that married couples do lead them together with the appropriate expertise.

Recapitulation: abilities to be fostered

The skills required of those who lead are the same abilities that marriage education is designed to foster. Leaders have to start by recognising and affirming ways in which people ordinarily relate well are able to cope with personal differences, and perceive and deal with the realities in a situation sensibly. Leaders have to demonstrate these skills in an unaffected way themselves and they will arrange their programme so as to have scope to do this. The way they work together and the ways in which they interact with the people taking part are an essential ingredient. They are showing communication skills in being able to listen and attend to someone else, recognising personal feelings and responding clearly to what others say and do.[7] These skills depend on a capacity for empathy, an ability to recognise another person's experience separately from one's own, and the integrity to accept it without taking it from them. This integrity is important; it is easily overlooked, as, for example, when preachers appropriate stories from people's lives and give them a twist of their own. Here the leader has to avoid the trap of distorting or twisting someone else's experience to fit his own theories.

When people speak about themselves and about what they know of friendship and family life, they show how they have learned to make sense of their experience. Through prompted conversation they may recognise a view of themselves in relation to others, from which they see how to respond more clearly and consistently to someone they are close to. That relationship can be further enhanced when both people can recognise and respond more adequately to anxieties and matters of concern either may be aware of. Being able to enter into another's experience, even partially, is the basis for that kind of mutual communication. Because it is often done without words, this kind of learning includes gesture and body language. It may seem pretentious to suggest that these lifeskills need to be taught to couples embarking on marriage. Yet many will not have acquired them and some marriages run into early difficulty because couples do not know how to communicate effectively. Those who are highly educated may need as much help in this as those who have grown up in very restricted circumstances. Nor can it be assumed that couples who want to run marriage preparation courses for others are skilful in these ordinary ways.

In conjoint work a minister will need to be able to facilitate dialogue between the two partners and observe and describe to them patterns of behaviour they might usefully recognise. This will also mean being ready to tolerate anxiety and anger and deal with conflict, and to support partners in doing so. When working with groups, leaders will need additional skills for initiating and maintaining activity and interaction between group members. Clearly there is a difference between the ability to lead a discussion on an agreed topic and that needed to manage the way a group of people share personal experience and learn from it.[8] As leaders grow in understanding and skill, they should be better able to gauge what they can do.

Let us assume that a man and woman are working together to lead a group of six couples meeting for a series of four sessions. They will need to clarify working differences or areas of conflict and deal with them. They will have to be able to stay in role and support each other in doing that. They will need to observe the way members of the group interact with them, with their partners and with others in the group, and use this knowledge to direct activities. The boundaries that are sought by group members will need to be perceived and the leaders may have to provide boundaries themselves. It will be their task to maintain a sequence to any directed activities and to determine what will be appropriate by responding to cues from participants.

Notes

1. Clulow, C. F., 'Children—For Better, For Worse?' in *Change in Marriage*, National Marriage Guidance Council, 1982. See also his book *To Have and to Hold*, Aberdeen University Press 1982.
2. *Marriage Matters*. A Consultative Document by the Working Party on Marriage Guidance (HMSO 1979), p. 80.
3. Most courses of this kind have been provided by the Churches but often with the support and expertise of other agencies. When local marriage guidance councils, rather than counsellors acting individually, have been asked to help in developing and managing courses of this kind, the results have generally been more thoroughly reported. An account of research by the National Marriage Guidance Council is given by Joy Ross in *Marital Therapy in Britain*, vol. 2, ed. Windy Dryden, 1986. The Catholic Marriage Advisory Council has developed courses nationally within the Catholic Church and sometimes for other local churches, and a useful summary of their approach is contained in *Your Future Begins Now* (two volumes, CMAC 1984).

4. Research in Canada by the Department of Family Social Science, University of Minnesota, suggests this. See for example Olson, D. H., 'How effective is marriage preparation?' in Mace, D., ed., *Prevention in Family Services*, Sage 1983.
5. See Olson, D., op. cit.
6. This is suggested by a personal study by Andrew Body based on his experience as incumbent of two Yorkshire parishes, and by an evaluation by Margaret Stevens of marriage preparation courses in a Nottingham parish.
7. There are a number of books about these skills. See for example Jacobs, M., *Swift to Hear*, SPCK 1985, and Murgatroyd, S., *Counselling and Helping*, Methuen 1985.
8. There is a good summary of groupwork principles in Murgatroyd, S., op. cit.. Experience can be gained using simple group skills in leading topic-based discussion; see for example, Grigor, J. C., *Building Relationships*, *Family Relationships*, and *Marriage Relationships*, Connections Series, Bible Society 1985 onwards. Material on working with groups of couples is to be found in: Stahmann, R. F., and Hiebert, W. J., *Premarital Counselling*, Lexington, MA: Lexington Books 1980; and Garland, D. S. R., *Working with Couples for Marriage Enrichment*, San Francisco: Jossey Bass 1983. Further material on groupwork includes: Douglas, T., *Groupwork Practice*, Tavistock (basic for social work); Kindred, M., *Once upon a group . . .* , privately published by the author (20 Dover Street, Southwell, Notts NG25 0EZ) 1987 (offers a simply illustrated guide to the skills and snares of group leadership); Open University Community Education Department, *Leading a Group*, Open University 1984, 1988 (a workshop of ten sessions for training people to use Community Education Packs in groups and includes excellent practical notes; Whitaker, D. S., *Using Groups to help people*, Routledge & Kegan Paul 1985 (detailed and comprehensive for social work and therapy); Smith, P. B., *Group Processes and Personal Change*, New York: Harper & Row 1980 (theory and practice in sensitivity training); and Egan, G., *Face to Face: the small-group experience and interpersonal growth*, Monterey, CA: Brooks/Cole 1973 (a working guide to small group processes). An excellent practical account of couples in group interactions is also given in Mace, D., *Close Companions*, New York: Continuum Books 1984, ch. 14.

EIGHT

Celebrating

The pastoral task is thus not mere instruction; it is more properly the bringing into focus of a vision, the enabling of two persons to see clearly, and to make their own, an image which is partly inside them—a creation of their own nascent love—and partly beyond them—something given from God who has from creation brought them as man and woman to be what they are, and to become the man and wife they would wish to be.[1]

Two ministers are talking about their dealings with couples getting married. They recognise that they are often trying to bridge a gap between the un-Christian assumptions and behaviour they see to be increasingly prevalent and their view that marriage is a God-given vocation of commitment and faithfulness to one's partner in a lifelong union. They want to be able, with these couples, to use the marriage service with integrity. They are aware too that at a first interview couples are sometimes embarrassed about asking for a church wedding, because they do not come to church. They think some are also wary of being censured for already living together.

Both these ministers would understand the reasoning that lies behind the previous two chapters: the value of the person-centred approach in both counselling and teaching, and the need to exercise something of those two roles. They are also aware of being ministers of the gospel, representing the Church's mission to draw people into a right relation with God. One of them does that by offering couples some instruction in the Christian faith so that each partner can decide whether they believe there is a Christian basis for their marriage. It is enough for one partner to know this, but where neither can assent to it, he believes it would be dishonest to proceed to the marriage service. The other minister is not so sure about this approach; there is a difficulty about prescribing what people should be expected to assent to. Many have come to Christian faith in their own time and through personal experience. Marriage is sacramental in that it is a means of grace through which people are renewed and glorified. But is it a sacrament only for those who are baptised?

Questions of this kind will arise in other contexts and the way ministers respond will depend on who they are as ministers, and not just on an isolated view of what they are about when people come to get married. Christian ministry is not simply a matter of conforming to certain clearly defined and permanent roles and rules but is a continuously changing work in which a number of roles and responsibilities, strands of thought and experience are integrated. It is a ministry of gospel that comes in the flesh, embodied and centred in persons, yet here and now confusing in its pluriformity. As ministers reflect theologically on this ministry they depend on a Christian tradition in many forms, expressed through Scripture and liturgy, spirituality and ethics. They possess the experience they have gained in community with others, and they can pay attention to the insights, ideas and information of contemporary cultures and disciplines.[2] Clearly they do not consciously do that every time someone knocks on the door to get married, but their response to each request will make more sense if it is part of that continuing reflection, something that may be hard to sustain in the face of indifference and practical obstacles.

The privacy of believing

Religious beliefs, for all their outward manifestation, are well protected from investigation and intrusion. People who stoutly resist any suggestion that they should talk about their convictions or become identified with a particular church have deep-rooted attitudes to support them. Any minister can expect to encounter resistance because people do not wish to discuss what they believe. One priest described this experience very graphically: 'All's going well and then you mention Christian marriage and the blinds come down.' Couples may be expecting the minister to talk about religion, that is his job, but they do not have to fall for it. They are defending their personal freedom to choose, just as I do when a salesman calls at my house. Someone who wants to sell me something I do not need, or convert me from my present way of life, is a threat and may make me feel uncomfortable. A couple feeling under that kind of pressure from a minister may act politely and let him say his piece, particularly if they are in his home, but they will naturally resist conversion.

The distraction of religion

There may be occasions when one partner or both will respond gladly to a clear statement on the lines that 'You have to be a believer in order to enjoy marriage in its fullness'. Without denying that many Christians might believe this to be true, it can very obviously become a self-authenticating statement. In the process of getting married some people may be looking for a new or altered frame of reference which will bring stability to the chaos and uncertainty they may be experiencing. They may be looking for a way of reordering a past that they find disquieting. These are genuine needs and aspirations which have to be attended to; but men and women who experience an apparent religious conversion at the time of their marriage, may unconsciously want to avoid addressing the task of getting married. In these circumstances the minister has to hold to that primary task of helping the couple test the integrity of their intentions. It is easy to be distracted by overt religious behaviour, whereas if it is simply and warmly acknowledged it will find its own expression later. If the convictions are well-founded, there will be time later to nurture them. On the face of it, this may seem perverse. Someone keen to become a Christian at the time of their marriage would expect a minister, if no one else, to take them seriously. Yet these new-found convictions will soon need to be understood and lived out in marriage, and the minister has to use the opportunity to engage both partners in looking at that. In this way he will be treating the matter of faith seriously by focusing on the task in hand.

So getting religious, rather like becoming totally concerned with the practical arrangements and trappings of the wedding, can be a cautionary sign that a person or a couple may be avoiding the personal issues referred to in earlier chapters: the physical, social, mental and sexual factors. Those who are professing Christians may show the same inclination to sidetrack any encouragement to explore their behaviour together as a couple. There may of course be other reasons for this: not wanting to risk condemnation from the minister or a reluctance to talk of such intimate matters with someone they are accustomed to know and see regularly in the context of worship and prayer. They might be much more willing to have such a conversation with another person who is less well known to them. Much as we might try to remove inhibitions about talking of sexual and intimate matters in the context of Christian ministry it is sensible to recognise the boundaries that others may wish to provide for themselves, at least initially.

We may also have to acknowledge that the moral basis (or the lack of it) on which others have made decisions about their sexual behaviour, is inconsistent with Christian teaching. If I have begun this ministry with couples by acknowledging while not judging their intentions, because I consider it the wisest way of working with them, I may have to make it clear at some point that I am neither condemning nor condoning their behaviour. Where one partner has regrets about the past he or she may be moved to acknowledge them and possibly express them penitently. Yet whether or not that happens because as a minister I am consistent and trustworthy, is a matter of providence. There can be a conflict of roles here; I have chosen to exercise several which held together can be mutually effective.

Couples who wish to relate their experience of domestic life, love and sex, and their expectations of marriage to the Christian faith may be helped to do that by exploring the meaning Christians have given to the phrase 'marriage in the Lord'. It refers to marriages between partners who allow the knowledge that they are living in Christ to determine their behaviour in marriage. Keen to bear witness to that conviction they may choose a reading for their marriage from one of the New Testament letters (e.g. Eph. 5.21 – 33). It may be useful to talk with them about the family rules that are affirmed there, recognising their social origin and the way in which Christian discipleship transcends culture and particular household forms; about the way authority and care are found already in their relationship and can be exercised in marriage, inwardly and outwardly. Nor is marriage enjoined on all; Jesus and Saint Paul both spoke of those who renounce it for the sake of the kingdom. Those who live in Christ may have to test their vocation in different ways; what the bond of marriage represents to the whole community of faith is God's faithfulness and forgiveness. Those are two marks that Christians have looked for in all relations that are 'in Christ', in and out of marriage.

The phrase 'Christian marriage' is used to mean different things; it can create confusion as well as unity. It unites many who wish to maintain the qualities of exclusiveness, commitment and permanence that are inherently part of marriage in Christian terms. The confusion arises because you do not have to be baptised or a practising Christian to aspire to or enjoy such a marriage. Thus the phrase might be narrowly restricted to describing a marriage between two Christians (choosing how you define them), or more widely applied to those who marry intending 'Christian marriage'. This wider definition would in theory apply to those marrying according to English law in register offices or churches. Prior to celebrating a marriage a minister needs to talk to a couple about their understanding of marriage so that they can recognise whether their intentions match the ritual. In this respect, taking the wider definition, the law and Christian teaching point to a common understanding. The couple will be asked to say publicly that they commit themselves to one another, intending to be faithful to one another within a lawful and lifelong marriage.

Kindling faith

There will be many ways of exploring with others their sense of marriage and on the journey we may often be at loss for words or unable to come close to someone else's experience. People will sometimes be articulating ideas in words, sometimes responding in the imagination to symbols and images, and sometimes learning through their emotions and common experience. A single illustration can only hint at what this may involve.

Suppose a minister is in conversation with a couple who speak willingly about the love each partner feels for the other. They talk about being accepted, being wanted and at times being looked up to. The minister brings to this conversation the perspective of someone who recognises that the couple's experience of 'being accepted, warts and all' may help them to understand how grace and forgiveness create acceptance. That in accepting one another we are moved by the love of the one who first loved us. He will not expect them to complete this step all at once, but the conversation will be another signpost on their marital journey. Later on he may give them to read 1 John 4.7 – 12, as a possible lesson to have at their marriage service.

Signposts do not compel, people may choose to ignore them, but the helpful thing is to provide them where people may be expected to look for them, and to let them be pointers to what they are actually looking for. Journeys have to be made one step at a time. This way of teaching is often described as indirect and it suits the way many people acquire knowledge through living experience. It is akin to trial and error. As a method of communicating the Christian experience of God, it is, in the words of Søren Kierkegaard, characteristically and deliberately a 'deceit'!

> What then does it mean 'to deceive?' It means that one does not begin directly with the matter one wants to communicate, but begins by accepting the other man's illusion as good money, so one does not begin thus: I am a Christian; you are not a Christian.[3]

We may resist this deceit if we are sure that we have to proclaim Christianity directly and unequivocally, but in so doing we may deceive ourselves about the effectiveness of direct communication for this purpose. To pursue

Kierkegaard's deceit means starting off by being prepared to lose the prize. It is to begin by saying, let us talk about your view of life and love rather than starting by talking about my view of Christianity. And the risk of love can be like that; lovers who surrender themselves by first accepting the one they love rather than seeking first to be accepted, risk losing all.

To this way of ministry I bring not my expertise about marriage or Christianity but my sense of who I am and what I know, and my willingness to be a learner, a disciple too. If I am to teach not by instructing but by enabling people to explore experience and articulate their attitudes and feelings, I need to be doing the same thing myself. As I am helping a couple to discover what marriage means to them, and to see how their understanding may be changing, so I need to be open to the change in myself.

Going through the service

The preparation for their marriage service can be grounded in what partners will share of their own relationship. A minister who goes straight to a perusal of the form of service without engaging in the necessary preliminary conversation will be starting cold. It may never have been realistic to assume a couple were familiar with the shape and wording of the service and many generations of ministers have generally taken time to go through the service with them. Those who are regular worshippers may find it relatively easy to recognise the rite that is provided, but even so they will need to make it their own. For all its quality of timelessness and capacity to stir human imagination, the service may for many be an occasion detached from their experience of life and love, carrying echoes of a past that is not part of their history. The aim of this preparation is to assist the couple to know that 'this is happening to us'.

By listening to them and helping the partners to share their aspirations and invest the words they will use with the knowledge of their own experience, the minister will begin this process. It is not just a matter of the partners beginning to understand the meaning of the service; at the same time the words and actions of the rite have to be filled out with the knowledge of what they as man and woman think and feel. The process is as emotional as it is intellectual. And later the rehearsal for the wedding will be an essential stage in the process.

In studying the service, certain items call for attention. Firstly the words. Providing a selection of readings and prayers and asking the partners to make a choice together in their own time, is an obvious way of asking many of them to prepare. Churches allow their ministers to create and adapt the form of service in different ways. Those who have some freedom over the use of words may on occasions encourage a couple to compose their own parts of the service. Choice of service versions will sometimes make it possible for partners to recognise by comparison the form they want to use. The wording of the vows and the choice between alternatives can be understood by building on earlier conversations about the partners' own experience of faithfulness and personal commitment, and their sense of roles and responsibilities. Couples will also vary in the way they want to say their vows; many feel more comfortable repeating them after the minister whereas some actually want to speak them to one another directly. The different options can be sensitively explored.

Not all couples will want to read much and the minister may simplify the options. By the time he starts to discuss service details, he is likely to have gained some insight into the way each couple relate and how much they aspire to what is often referred to as a 'companionate' rather than a 'traditional' marriage, and how comfortable they will feel about the active role they have to play in the rite.

The minister can bring to this conversation a view of the way the English vows have evolved. The questions a priest asked of a couple eight hundred years ago were then an innovation in order to establish *their* consent, in place of parental permission. The priest asked the questions (recognisably those which begin 'Will you . . .' in contemporary forms) and the couple had a largely passive role: they answered. Within a few hundred years, couples were taking an active part as well, making their vows by plighting their troth to one another in the present tense, 'I take thee . . .'. Modern services have further heightened the active roles of the two partners, as much in the way the rite is presented as in what they are expected to say and do. This development has now affected the mutuality of their roles. Bride and groom may express equal standing before each other and recognise mutual responsibilities. The status of the bride and the role of her father in giving her to be married, may also be less accentuated.

The words and the silence should be supported by the music that is chosen. The minister is not there to present his own preferences but to offer some experience of pitfalls to avoid. It might, for example, be necessary to remove any idea that it is solely the bride's prerogative to choose hymns and music, or that it is the couple's decision taken without acknowledging the capacity of the congregation. This is not simply a matter of whim. Just as the minister is hoping that both partners will recognise the rite as theirs, he has also to help others to be part of it as well: parents, for whom it is in a sense a rite of letting go, and others for whom it may be a rite of affirmation, renewal or mourning. Music carries a great deal of personal emotion and may evoke memories far more powerfully than words.

Physical actions and movements are as important as words and music; ceremony, however simple, focuses attention and helps people to recognise what is happening to them. Effective ritual engages the imagination and the actions assist participants to internalise the sense of the change they are undergoing, the resolutions they are making, and the responsibilities they are discharging or acquiring. The task is not to 'explain' the ritual (the reasons we give may be boringly rational, as though to counter vain superstition), but to enable people to carry out their own actions. Our understanding of ritual, however well informed by a study of liturgy, will come too from our pastoral experience of it. Ideally any academic study should acquaint us with the social and cultural setting and the historical circumstances in which marriage rites have taken shape and been revised.[4] Then we learn to see what is happening today as a bride and groom stand before a minister, against the background of what has been happening socially to marriage relations.

Conversation about the service would lead naturally into a rehearsal, but there has to be time for the couple to talk together on their own about any options they can exercise, to read through forms of service and preferably make decisions with some insight into the expectations of their families and friends. The minister will determine any limits to the variations they can consider and there will probably have to be time for relaxed negotiation. Sometimes at the rehearsal, a partner may have second thoughts about some of the arrangements, or the minister may be aware that something does not feel right. When the rehearsal is a few days before the wedding, it may be easier to be flexible.

Rehearsal

This can be a reassuring occasion once people have become accustomed to the strange atmosphere of the empty church. A couple may also gain more familiarity with the building by coming to a service beforehand, such as when their banns are read. At the rehearsal both partners need to apprehend something of what they will be doing as well as saying.

This means savouring the movement and the spaces in the rite, and recognising where and how they will be positioned. To make the point very practically, it is worth taking a lot of time to rehearse the actual movements of standing and kneeling, turning to each other and walking together, so that the partners feel in charge of their own actions as well as being responsible for what they say. How this is to be achieved will vary from couple to couple. Some will feel more like being in charge than others and in their own unique way; how each partner treats the other will express something of how they relate as a couple.

When should the rehearsal be and who needs to attend it? There may be advantages in not only the bride and groom being there but also some members of the family, the best man and the bridesmaids. If the wedding is going to be an organised family occasion in which everybody wants to participate and if the couple themselves are clearly looking forward to this, a large rehearsal can be a valuable occasion. Everybody involved will have the opportunity to experience this final preparation and identify with what is going to happen. At the same time the minister will gain a great deal of insight into the family expectations of the occasion and have a chance to become better known to the family. Because those who have parts to play will be concerned to know exactly what they have to do, the minister will have to attend to them all and in the process the particular needs of the bride and groom may get overlooked. Unless they are very at ease, they may be inhibited about raising any particular uncertainties or doubts about what they have to do.

It will often be more appropriate to ask the couple to come for the rehearsal on their own. The minister can give them his undivided attention and their responsibility will also be heightened. They will become the ones who have to tell others with a part to play what it is they have to do, albeit in the knowledge that any last-minute queries can be dealt with by the minister on the day. Rehearsing the couple on their own is likely to encourage them to feel more in charge.

The officiant's task on the day

People getting married generally feel nervous beforehand because they want the occasion to go smoothly. The wedding ceremony is the part about which many will be most anxious. The minister is likely to be carrying some of that anxiety, particularly if he has invested time in preparing for it and wants the occasion to be one the couple will enjoy and remember. The responsibility for ensuring that all goes well may be keenly felt as the service begins and the minister faces the congregation and the couple, when any signs of nervousness are all too visible. The officiant's role calls for dignity without stiffness and requires that he be sensitive to the couple without being distracted by them. The preparation shared in by minister and couple beforehand may help them to feel some affinity as a team on the day. A minister who has to officiate at the wedding of a couple he has not met is at a disadvantage, and so too are the couple.

All this takes place 'in the face of this congregation' and for the couple this means 'our families and friends', those who have been invited for the celebration. In the eyes of the minister the guests can all too easily seem like just another wedding congregation, a sea of faces largely unknown who will be unfamiliar with the service and possibly unimpressed by previous experience of the Church and its ministers. The congregation can easily become a distraction, a crowd of people to be preached to, impressed, or somehow befriended with expansive bonhomie. Yet the minister's relationship with the congregation, unless many of them are already known to him, is through the couple and by upholding the couple in their task he builds trust too with those others who are present.

The decision about whether or not to give an address needs to be carefully weighed. A thoughtful consideration of circumstances is called for,[5] not an invariable rule; but if the minister knows he is equipped to say something simply and naturally, it might be done best when those present will have settled down enough to hear it. That is likely to be after the marriage, and before the prayers or a communion. At such a point an address would give the couple a breathing space and time to become aware of their feelings while momentarily not the centre of attention (they will need seats in a comfortable place). An evangelistic sermon is out of place in what is first and foremost a celebration with bridegroom and bride. A good address will be one that is consonant with the mood of the occasion. Something spoken from inside the ritual to those who are assisting at it. Something said not just to the couple but to everyone. What still needs saying that has not already been said by the rite? The aim might be to connect the uniqueness of each couple to some of that experience of marriage the minister perceives to be present in people's minds, and in that way to draw out what the rite already says and shows of marriage. It will be the minister's own total sense of what marriage and love is, what he feels as well as thinks, that will fill out any words he chooses.

The trio of church, marriage service and minister, will be parenting not just the couple but to some degree all who are present: all three work together. The building creates its own atmosphere and will engender certain feelings in the congregation as they wait for the service to begin. They will show those feelings by the way they behave. Hushed voices, embarrassed gestures and nervous laughter may be the signs of disarray. Relaxed silence or quiet conversation, unhurried movements and affectionate greetings are clues that people feel at home. By being present in the church before the service, by greeting the parents or close family of the bride and groom as they arrive, and by deliberately talking to them to put them at their ease, the minister may communicate a relaxed mood to them, which they will in turn convey to others. The minister is unlikely to know or wholly understand the way these families tick, but among those whom he greets will be the natural parents of the day, those respected figures in the family from whom others will take their cue and whose trust it is valuable to secure.

The service, like the church building, is part of the givenness. The minister who has worked with the couple beforehand to shape their rite will have the advantage of knowing that the service is going to be personal. Yet it is also the church's celebration of marriage and this is conveyed by the form and language. Individuals have their preference for 'thee' or 'you', but there is a blend of timelessness and immediacy that depends on elements other than the words themselves that are less obvious. The resonance of the service lies in the hopes that it carries and the memories that are evoked; good liturgy grows out of human experience and draws the knowledge of previous generations into the consciousness of the living. The officiant will do well to allow the service to do its own work. By being aware of its inclusiveness and proper ambiguity and leaving unsaid those things that need not be spoken, a minister may believe that his best performance lies in not getting in the way. He too is a guest.

Notes

1. From *Marriage, Divorce and the Church*, Report of the Archbishop's Commission on the Christian Doctrine of Marriage, SPCK 1971, p 53.
2. I derive these elements from Whitehead, J. D., and Whitehead, E. E., *Method in Ministry*, New York: Seabury 1980, in which is clearly described a method of attending to and asserting these three elements in the course of theological reflection. These authors have also written *Marrying Well: Stages on the Journey of Christian Marriage*, New York:

Doubleday 1981, a valuable and practical illustration of their method applied to learning in marriage.

3. Kierkegaard S., *The Point of View,* quoted by Tinsley E. J., in 'Tell it Slant', *Theology,* May 1980.

4. Stevenson, K., *Nuptial Blessing*, Alcuin Club/SPCK 1982, provides a comprehensive study of the rites of Eastern and Western Christendom. An exploratory commentary on the ASB Marriage Service is given in Jasper, R. C. D., and Bradshaw, P. F., *A Companion to the Alternative Service Book,* SPCK 1986. Advice about the presentation of the rite is provided by Perham, M., in *Liturgy Pastoral and Parochial*, SPCK 1984.

5. Bunting, I., *Preaching at Weddings,* Grove Worship Series no. 74, 1980, offers a good consideration of the issues and has some useful suggestions, in addition to well-grounded comments about marriage services.

NINE

Moving On

This ministry with two people intending to marry may often seem like an intervention detached from other work and relationships. It may be difficult to root it in any recognisable common ground or relate it to other activities. This will not be true every time; at least one of the partners and the members of his or her family may be known to the minister or members of the congregation. Yet it does seem to be increasingly the case that this occasional office feels like a 'one-off', made familiar only by the demand to attend not to one or two couples a year but perhaps twenty, and in some churches many more. Those who enjoy taking weddings and feel a keen sense of the importance of giving marriages an encouraging start may not have any doubt about wanting to do this work, but what holds others back is the apparent futility of time spent, after which the couple are never seen again.

Keeping in touch

The kind of relationship a couple develop with the church where they marry, assuming they are not already members of the congregation, will be affected by the frequency with which they have contact with people at the church during the time before their wedding. It may be a relationship primarily with one minister or it may be shared with a number of people who take an interest in them and become involved in their marriage preparations. Yet these relations are likely to lapse if the couple live elsewhere after their marriage, unless steps are taken by different people to stay in touch. Where some form of marriage follow-up can be arranged to which couples are pleased to come, continuing contact for a year or so may be very effective. Yet couples may need to move on and establish roots where they intend settling down for a length of time. Often this sense of putting down roots comes not when they marry but when they become parents. At this stage, encouraging the couple to relate to the church where they live rather than where they married can be the best course of action.

A couple may value receiving a periodic greeting from the church where they married, particularly if it evokes grateful memories of good pastoral support. The knowledge that they are being remembered may encourage them as they cope with some of the adjustments of early marriage and on visits home they may be glad to renew acquaintance. The value of maintaining contact for a short while at least is that it can make it easier to commend the couple to the church near their new home at a time when it may mean more to them. Commendations immediately following a wedding are often difficult to follow up when the couple themselves have still to adjust to their move and have yet to emerge from the often intense mutual absorption of early marriage. Left to judge for themselves if and when they want to make new links with the church, they might find it easier if they were given some form of introduction such as a postcard from the minister who married them, addressed in an open way with space for the couple to put in their own current address. They could deliver it or send it to the minister of their choice when they were ready to be visited and become known.

Maintaining course

The aim of keeping in touch is not to hang on to the couple but to strengthen their own sense of the grace that is in them. It is for the affirmation of their marriage and it will probably mean something if the ministry they enjoy before their wedding carries a sense of realism, and gets beneath the surface to the important task of assisting both partners emotionally as well as physically to leave their parents behind and become morally and spiritually one. This change of identity is not brought about as quickly as the public change of status.

The making of the marriage bond is unconscious as well as conscious, and observation shows how much the early months and years of marriage are critical. The inner yearning to 'go home to Mum' is often denied; when one of the spouses decides to do just that it can provoke a firm reaction from parents which makes it quite clear that this is no longer home. Parents and their children often take time to work through this transition. Regular visits to each set of parents, sometimes more complicated when they have divorced, are a way of allowing time for this adjustments. Parents look for the assurance that the couple are getting on alright; the new spouses may be checking that the parents are surviving without them. Each may also keep in touch with old friends and be glad to enjoy some of the home comforts they forgo because of the way their spouse does things differently. Of course things are not always like this. Either partner may be very relieved to get away from home and have little desire to go back on visits. If the partners differ in this respect, with only one of them maintaining warm relations with the family, the imbalance may become a source of envy and even jealousy. Through continuing the contact they have with the parents, ministers may become aware of these tensions and help the parents to respond sensitively to them. The displacement of loyalties and the strengthening of the new attachment may then be helped indirectly by the influence ministers have in a general way.

The Church has a parenting role that is partially symbolised in the marriage rite when a father places his daughter's hand in the priest's before it is then taken by the bridegroom as he makes his vows, an action that needs to be thought of as mirrored on the bridegroom's side. In this mutual transfer of attachments and authority our task is to enable parents and children alike to take leave so that there is space and freedom for the new marriage to grow. They will learn from experience that this leaving and cleaving occurs not just in the marriage rite but in a succession of incidents and acts often spanning many years. The Church's continuing ministry, like the marriage rings, is to remind them of the vow and covenant 'they have made this day'. The Church's continuing influence in the lives of their parents can similarly encourage them to affirm this new bond and recognise how they can allow their relationship with their children to be re-formed. Many parents will also find this to be a transition in which they too have to come together again as a couple.

The ministry we undertake at a marriage is in the context of the interactions and continuing life course of each generation. A very clear explanation of the relationship between pastoral care and the life cycle has been provided by two authors. Herbert Anderson[1] outlines the primary transitional task at each of five stages from marriage until the time the last child leaves home. The family exists for three purposes: for procreation, to be a stabilising community and for the individuation of its members. In its structure it needs to adapt to change, encourage interdependence among those who belong to it or who remain open to its environment, and allow for diversity. A family functions effectively through a combination of flexible roles, adaptable rules and dependable rituals. Donald Capps,[2] using Erik Erikson's life cycle theory, examines the various roles that ministers can undertake to support a person's development at different stages. Both authors show the way in which this particular ministry at the time of a marriage can be rooted in ordinary ground. By taking it seriously the minister improves his own capacity to engage in that ordinary ministry. The couples he meets are given a chance to recognise and develop their marriage and family-building capacity, the attitudes and abilities, that will make a reality of their intentions.

As the couple move on, so the Church's ministry with them moves into another stage. Yet many of the activities and tasks outlined in these chapters will be uncompleted and of continuing relevance. Out of this experience of ministry with couples at the time of their wedding we learn ways of being a support to people at other times in their marriage. It will be a ministry to those who move in and settle in our community alongside those who are the parents of the couples who move away.

Notes

1. Anderson, H., *The Family and Pastoral Care*. Philadelphia: Fortress Press, 1984.
2. Capps, D., *Life Cycle Theory and Pastoral Care*. Philadelphia: Fortress Press, 1983.

Part Three

TEN

Personality, Marriage and Ministry

The practical methods outlined in Part Two will depend on a minister being allowed to draw on partners' personal experience. This experience will often be conveyed more by the way they behave and treat each other than in what they actually say to him directly. To begin with some generalisations about marriage as an institution, and the social and cultural aspects of getting married (as presented in Part One), may fit particular partners. It may be easy, for example, to recognise where they belong socially and culturally. As he gets to know each couple a minister may become aware of some of the factors in their relationship which will give stability to their marriage. This is when their personal expectations of marriage, sense of marital roles and ways of behaving with one another come more clearly into view. Through the minister's observations the partners may discern something of the potential shape and dynamics of their marriage. His own theoretical understanding of marriage as a relationship, and his ability to relate it to what he sees going on, will provide the minister with a valuable framework for his conversations and directed activity. This chapter offers a theoretical outline of the way men and women interact on different conscious and unconscious levels as they become married. From this it may also be clearer how a minister can find himself part of that interaction.

Three sub-systems or levels of a marriage

The exercise 'Factors that contribute to a successful marriage' provided at the end of chapter 2 contains a list. When people are asked to place those factors in order of importance, three groupings generally emerge: cultural, background and personal, in that increasing order of importance. The personal factors contribute most in the long term to an intimate relationship.

The psychiatrist and marital therapist Henry Dicks wrote that the strength of a marriage bond depends on 'an overall positive balance of satisfactions over dissatisfactions for both partners'[1]. He recognised three sub-systems or levels of interaction which give stability and strength to the marriage bond. While factors at one level can be seen to relate to factors at another level, each sub-system can be regarded as having an independent and varying effect on the overall stability of the marriage. The three sub-systems he defined form the basis of the following description. It provides a view of marriage as a relationship and a way of recognising the level of intimacy at which a minister may be working with a couple.

Level one:
social and cultural factors

Although young people emphasise less than older generations today the desirability of partners sharing the same religious and political beliefs as a good basis for marriage, there is still an overall tendency in this country for people to marry within or close to their own social (occupational) class. Educational background, wealth and place of work have, until recently, largely determined the extent to which people of similar or different backgrounds will meet and socialise in order to begin friendships. Young people able to move away from home to pursue careers and those who take advantage of leisure and recreational opportunities that are increasingly less affected by class, have been more likely to meet those with different socio-cultural backgrounds from their own.

When two people decide to marry and begin to make arrangements, they may then discover how much cohesion there is between them at this first level. When they share similar ambitions and identify easily with each other's parental values and family norms, it will be easier to plan their marriage without a great deal of conflict. In the eyes of the public they will seem compatible. A minister who maintains his relationship with the couple at this level may be doing what the partners and their families expect. Benignly exercising a traditional role he might well be supported by convention and a social stability that will make further intervention unnecessary. Yet there is less of that social stability about and the partners themselves may be aware of the importance of their personal investment in the marriage if it is to survive.

Level two:
personal norms and behaviour

A person develops a sense of individual identity by attempting to live by personal beliefs and values, testing acquired norms and models of behaviour, learning to make conscious judgements and forming hopes and expectations. The young question the attitudes and behaviour they have learnt at home or from adults in *loco parentis* as part of this process of finding their own identity. Sometimes the struggle will be about superficial matters of dress, manners and freedom from supervision; at other times it will be a much deeper rebellion against norms and standards that are at odds with the ascending sense of self. Rather like the rock climber, the one making this ascent finds occasional opportunities for a pause before making the next move. They will be safe places where for the time being he can keep his balance, where his beliefs and outward behaviour can be compatible. Friendships, comfortable peer groups, and organisations offer a temporary staging post or port in a storm. For some this will be provided by Christian allegiance. A person may now be ready to choose who to be intimate with and how far they will go. The most attractive partnership may develop into a long-term commitment or a marriage.

As a relationship deepens partners will become more aware of the match between their expectations and what is actually happening between them; for it to be comfortable there needs to be consistency of two kinds. Firstly, each partner has to find the other's behaviour acceptable and in accord with what he or she is looking for in the partnership. Thus the demands each makes upon the other, conscious decisions on matters of importance and actual behaviour as male and female at an ordinary and intimate level, will affect each person's perception of the match. Secondly, each partner has to feel comfortable with the way the partnership looks from outside, its public face and overtly shared expectations and activities, along with the way it affects other friendships and family ties.

In the kind of ministry that has been outlined it is to this level that much of the conversation and activity will be directed. The partners' personal norms and behaviour will become evident and so too will those of the minister. His non-judgemental behaviour is likely to encourage the partners to be open with each other. Yet he will sometimes feel uncomfortable with the way one or other of the partners behaves and he may disagree with some of their attitudes. There may be an opportunity for him to express this disagreement; for example when he is aware that it may help the two partners to consider a different point of view constructively. Yet the probability is that both partners will need some encouragement in the first place to be frank about themselves without fear of criticism. They may come expecting to be judged and be reluctant to give too much away.

In the relationship with each other also, each partner will initially be testing out how far their own consciously held values and patterns of behaviour are acceptable. The longer the relationship continues and gains a strength of its own and the more each invests in the partnership, the more both will find it possible to adapt their behaviour to each other and to give and take in order to survive as a couple. Recognising feelings evoked by unfamiliar kinds of role behaviour, consciously agreeing or making accommodation on specific matters, dealing with and negotiating expressed wishes—all these day-to-day activities provide early evidence of the potential in the partnership for this long-term growth. Their conversation with the minister may be somewhat like their own courtship in that respect, cautiously testing out reactions before they disclose too much and risk losing the friendship.

From the way they treat him, the minister may discern something of their openness with each other.

Tolerance and flexibility will help partners adapt to changing conditions and needs, and sustain a long-lasting union. Personal values will become increasingly evident and affect the extent to which they can pursue shared goals and how far they can agree to differ. A divergence of interests as time goes on need not mean the break-up of the relationship. On the contrary, it can be deepened when each partner can affirm the other in their distinctiveness. Only when early common interests decline and changed personal values no longer sustain the mutual bond, does a couple grow apart at this personal level. In such circumstances parting may be a very rational business, conducted with a dignity that enables both partners to continue to have ordinary dealings with each other. What is nevertheless evident at the time of a separation is distress, and to understand that it is necessary to recognise a third sub-system in which emotional factors arise at an unconscious level.

Level three:
individual unconscious factors

According to psychodynamic theory it is past experiences of being in a relationship with other significant people (family, close friends, lovers), that come into play as we form new relationships. This is part of the attraction that men and women hold for one another, and its unconscious basis may not be realised until people share this experience through interacting in an intimate way and release memories and associated feelings. In a sustained sexual relationship, the intimate bond between two partners is affected by the emotional experience of their respective childhoods and in particular by the effect of relations with their parents and others close to them. It is the mix of needs and capacities brought by each partner which in the long term has a lot to do with the quality of their marriage.

An apparently good match based on a comfortable fit at the other two levels can become problematic. Two people from

similar backgrounds, competent at their work and enjoying a
range of easy social relations, become attracted and marry.
Even a sensible consideration of their mutual expectations
does not uncover the unconscious relational needs each is
still seeking to deal with. These may soon have to be dealt
with and can often be met because each partner has in
sufficient measure the capacity to love and tolerate the other
through the further developmental process needed. They may
have unconsciously chosen each other in order to do this,
unerringly matching complementary needs and capacities.
Experience connects with experience at this unconscious level.
Partners may be drawn to one another through the unspoken
message that they have experienced a similar grief, or both
enjoy a particular pleasure. There is a sense in which some of
these personal encounters with other people could be called
'meetings of memories'. This phenomenon is illustrated by a
training exercise used by family therapists and described by
Robin Skynner.[2]

At an early stage, when the people involved in training are
still relative strangers, they are brought together as a group
and asked to pair off by choosing someone who either makes
them think of a person in their family or gives them the
feeling that they would have filled a gap in their family.
They are also asked not to speak to one another while they do
this. When the choice has been made and they have paired,
they talk together to see what made them pick each other.
The sequence is then repeated so that the pairs form fours;
the four together start to find out about each other. Invariably
they discover that they all come from families that 'function
in very similar ways'. In other words, they come from families
in which it was difficult to show affection, or in which anger
was rarely expressed, or which had experienced the loss of
someone in a similar way.

That example illustrates the sense in which marriage is a
return home. As a basis for his description of the unconscious
behaviour that comes into play as two partners attempt to
deepen the attachment between them, Henry Dicks used
object relations theory. It offers a psychodynamic description
of what seems to be happening at an unconscious level in
intimate relationships where there is strong attraction or

attachment. (There is an outline of this theory in Appendix D.)[3] Marriage offers a context in which individuals can continue to use the resources of love and tolerance they have already developed. They may also be trying to satisfy relational needs that have been repressed or split off in earlier relationships. One may be attractive to the other 'because he or she promises or represents a rediscovery of an important lost aspect of the subject's own personality, which, owing to earlier conditioning, had been recast as an object for attack or denial.'[4] The presence of these latent factors may support or contradict the integrity of a person's conscious reasons for marrying and influence how far they can satisfactorily seek and maintain comfortable relations with a partner. In the intensity of courtship these latent factors are often obscured, but they emerge in the new setting of the marriage and affect the new marital roles.

Using these three levels

Dicks concluded that an enduring marriage requires a good fit at two of these levels at least; two of the marital sub-systems have to function in a way that results in satisfaction to both partners. Strong agreements over personal norms and values supported by the deeper unconscious fit can bridge a wide socio-cultural distance in the first sub-system. And strong affinity at this first level combined with congruent object-relations can cope with considerable overt personal differences over norms and values. The combination of a good fit without conflict in both of the first two levels may also be satisfactory where they provide a mutual defence against what lies unresolved at the third level. In this case much will depend on the capacity of each partner to regard the other as a whole person, on how benign these unconscious conflicts are, or on a quite complex and not always discernible collusion which brings its own rewards despite the apparent absence of love.

A minister may find that his interaction with the couple or one of the partners is taking place at the third level. If he has established a degree of rapport with them, some unconscious involvement is quite likely, but it may not be recognised. How far he intends to get involved will be determined by his sense of role. He may think it improper to let his own personality affect his ministry and so try to avoid this happening. He may limit what he says to generalisations and retain a formality in his dealings with others. Some couples may indicate very firmly that that is just what they prefer; they may be quick to recognise this to be the level at which he is most comfortable or decide that because he is the kind of person he is, this will be the level at which they will feel safe with him.

At any first meeting, social, cultural and religious affinity is likely to make for easier relations. Many clergy may be aware, for example, of how a culture gap can initially be an obstacle when they want to establish a rapport with a couple. The relationship begins to deepen when the minister invests in it something of himself, engaging with the couple at the level of his own feelings and attitudes and discovering common ground. This does not mean that he has to impose his own convictions and judgements on the couple, but rather that he has to be willing to be affected at this deeper level by the work he is doing. His own experience of intimate relations will connect with the experience of others; the 'meeting of memories' becomes a faculty, an instinct that the minister can use. It is a faculty he can be aware of through self-understanding and the emotional support others have given him to respond to his own feelings. Even when he is not aware of these connections and of his unconscious involvement with others, they may be at work; they may help or hinder his ministry. Psychiatrists and therapists use the concept of projective identification to describe these unconscious connections; the idea illuminates the way partners can be attracted to one another and the way in which a minister's unconscious self interacts with those he is interviewing.

Projective identification

When a person unconsciously denies feelings that cause him anxiety, the experience from which the psyche is defending itself remains repressed within the ego. ('Splitting' is the term used to define this—see Appendix D.) As long as the experience is too dangerous to deal with, a person may resist relations with someone else that threaten to unloose the associated feelings. That sounds dramatic but so too are the fantasies in which these psychological struggles are lived out in a person's inner world. The emotional resources used by the ego to guard the captive are not available for continuing dynamic growth and personal change. If however those feelings can be transferred to another object the internal threat can be lessened. So a person may be unconsciously looking for someone on whom to project these repressed feelings, to make that person the object of the experience, standing in place of the original object associated with it. In a sense it provides the psychic equivalent of the ritual scapegoat; the ego projects outside itself, laying on another object the experience it has been unable to come to terms with. This possibility is only realised when there is another object to receive the projection. The making of this connection is called projective identification.

How people actually manage to do this is not known, but the hypothesis provides an explanation that does seem to fit behaviour that has been observed under conditions of therapy. For example, a man who has repressed the grief experienced when a sister died during childhood may unconsciously recognise a partner who will grieve for him. If that second person has already repressed her own grief over a loss then she may end up carrying a double dose which becomes unbearable. Yet she cannot be relieved of it, because the partnership is being lived out around a collusion. If she rejects the projection she jeopardises the partnership.

Projective identification is a concept which

permits what goes on *between* people to be understood in terms of specific dynamic conflicts going on *within* them. For the conditions of projective identification to be met not only must there be a reciprocal exchange of projections but also there must be an active element in which one partner aims to evoke behaviour or feelings which have been repudiated from the self and is aided and abetted in this process by the other. In short, there must be collusion to sustain mutual projections.[5]

In therapeutic work with couples and families therapists try to recognise and use the projections that are placed on them. A minister too when working conjointly with a couple may become aware that he is experiencing something of the kind.

Consider as an illustration a priest interviewing a couple. The conversation between them seems inhibited and as the priest tries to encourage them to be more forthcoming he is conscious of feeling angry with the man. He is aware at the same time of feeling protective towards the woman. He gives his attention to the man, questioning him about why he wants to get married. Yet the more he attempts to do this, the more animated the woman becomes as she intervenes to answer the questions for her partner and moves closer to him. The priest wishes he could talk to the man on his own, and leans towards him; he wants to keep the couple apart and is about to tell the woman to stop interrupting.

It is possible to consider what is happening in that illustration by referring to the three different levels already described. On the face of it the couple seem to be curiously unsuited. The man is very untidy, almost slovenly, while the woman is neat, clean and carefully composed, and seems much more articulate. The priest may have been perplexed by this apparent mismatch and trying to make sense of it by his enquiry. At a deeper personal level he may have been responding with some annoyance and intolerance to a man who is very different from himself, untidy and seemingly careless. He may have considered it the man's role to answer his questions and not rely on his fiancée to come to his rescue. He may have been repelled by the idea of this woman marrying him. It is possible that something was also going on at an unconscious level; a clue to that is the way in which both the priest and the woman were physically drawing closer to the man and in different ways affecting one another's behaviour. The priest seeing that this was happening may have wondered whether the woman was reacting to his behaviour in this way because she wished to divert attention from her fiancé, or whether she was unconsciously treating him not as the priest but as someone else. He might have been able to test his idea that this was some kind of projection by asking her, 'Am I behaving like someone else you know, one of your family perhaps?' She might have not understood the question or been aware of such feelings or she might have replied that he did remind her of someone, her father.

The illustration is deliberately hypothetical and is not meant to imply that a minister should deliberately behave in a way that might encourage intense interaction. The point is that feelings are often aroused in interviews for conscious reasons as well as at an unconscious level. We are likely to find ourselves sometimes liking people and sometimes disliking them. When talking to a couple we may feel attracted to one of the partners, or enjoy a fantasy about being with one of them; we can be shocked by such feelings, and thrown off balance. The attraction may understandably be to do with someone's appearance—he may look like me or someone I love; or it may have something to do with the way we enjoy sparring together or are trying to impress each other. Such an unconscious attraction is something I may be able to use if I am not preoccupied with denying it, which can happen, particularly when the attraction is a sexual one.

When the attraction is not reciprocated, the projection is probably mine and provides a clue to relations in my own inner world. If on the other hand it is a mutual projection and if I am aware of it being reciprocal and I collude with it, I may be able to discover from my own feelings what is happening between the three of us. The question to ask myself is, What does this help me to understand about the relationship between the couple? It is their interaction that is the subject of attention. What is the interaction between the two partners doing at this moment to encourage this projection? Does it help me to see something about their own relationship or the past experience of one of them that I can usefully share with them? That is a possible approach I may be able to make use of only if I have some experience of my own projections. To work in that way should the occasion arise, I should also want afterwards to be able to consult someone qualified to take me through the experience and debrief me.

All that I bring . . .

All that I hold within myself and bring in different ways to this ministry may not always be clear to me. My own identity and its accumulated experience of my relations with others, will underlie the knowledge and skill acquired by study and training, and my sense of vocation and of God. Certainly the roles I have to perform are not impersonal functions. Within myself I hold together much that may be in conflict: an ambivalence about many things, a vision of the ideal and the experience of failure. That ambivalence, uncomfortable though it may be at times, may help me to tune into the experience of others. I shall be pulled in different directions by the work I do. I officiate at the weddings of those who seem to share few of my beliefs, I support and console a wife seemingly deserted by her husband though I sense why he may have found her hard to live with, and I celebrate the marriage of a woman I have known for years to a man who was divorced, well aware of the criticism of some of my colleagues. I recognise that my ministry will cause me difficulties of conscience that a clear sense of role will not altogether eliminate. The confusion will sometimes be augmented by changes in my personal circumstances and changing affections. An unexpected event, accident or personal crisis may upset my equilibrium; falling in love or discovering my partner's deceit can equally intrude on my ministry.

This experience is the very stuff of my ministry to those getting married, and in all charity is the antidote to their idealisations. By living with the tension between the way I wish things were and the way they are, I will be real to others. Idealisation is the unconscious defence against the experience I cannot live with. An idealisation of marriage is one wedding gift I would do without. Marriage in the New Testament is the subject of a number of paradoxical statements; the marriage of heaven and earth is announced but not yet perfected in my marriage. There is a truthfulness about the phrase 'a good enough marriage' that I am glad to take home.[6] Those who marry may need to be freed from an idealisation of each other and of marriage in order to become reliable companions and lovers. The dynamics of forgiveness maintain the momentum of change in marriage. 'The heartbeat of every marriage, as a Christian sees it, is forgiveness.'[7] This is the knowledge we may find ourselves sharing with those who come to be married; a vision of acceptance found within the love of God, caught sight of in the sparkle of human love and never quite lost in the shadows.

Notes

1. Dicks, H., *Marital Tensions*, Routledge & Kegan Paul, 1967, p. 129.
2. Skynner, R., and Cleese, J., *Families and how to survive them*, Methuen 1983, pp. 21, 22.
3. For a brief and lucid explanation of how object relations theory links with other theories used in marital work, see James, A. L., and Wilson, K., *Couples, Conflict, and Change,* 1983, chapter 3.
4. Dicks, H., op.cit. p. 30.
5. Clulow, C., *Marital Therapy, an inside view*, Aberdeen University Press, 1985, p. 44. This book provides a very clear illustration of the concept of projective identification along with a good account of object relations theory (pp. 43−50).
6. I first heard the phrase used by Moira Fryer, NMGC Tutor Consultant, during a lecture she gave in Bristol in 1984 on 'The New Partnership'. In D. W. Winnicott's idea of the 'good enough mother' is the hypothesis that to build an adequate nursing relation with her child the mother needs to be free from any unconscious idealisation of the mother figure resulting from her relations with her own mother.
7. Baker, J. A., *The Whole Family of God*, Mowbray 1981. From a sermon preached in Westminster Abbey, 1978.

Setting an Agenda

A Training Exercise

There is a great difference between what a couple might expect an interview with a minister to be about and what a minister might think they need to know before getting married. A group of ministers or potential leaders planning together might use a simple exercise to discover the range of different ideas they have about what a couple needs to know.

The Task

Consider the possible matters a couple might wish to raise under six different headings. Provide the list of headings and ask each person independently to list likely matters, as tasks seen from the couple's point of view.

The six headings relating to marriage are:

Physical aspects
Emotional aspects
Intellectual aspects
Social aspects
Sexual aspects
Spiritual aspects

(These headings are adapted from a list of five dimensions of need satisfied by marriage used by Dr Jack Dominian in *Marriage, Faith and Love* (Darton, Longman and Todd, 1981).

Allow an agreed time for people to make their own list and then share them in small groups. It is sometimes useful to collate the lists into one large one to show the range of items suggested.

From such an exercise individuals may recognise:

— how their own assumptions compare with those of others;
— that some of their assumptions are based on their own experience;
— that some matters seem to be commonly agreed;
— the range of issues that may arise in the course of working with many couples.

The purpose of the exercise is not to establish a core curriculum or basic syllabus, but to enable ministers to recognise the range of this work. It may encourage some to see teamwork and groupwork as useful options, alongside conjoint interviews, thus catering better for a combination of likely common needs and possible individual needs.

Possible matters to recognise

Here are examples of what collated lists of possible items could look like:

Physical

— to look at our expectations as to what we shall need in order to be satisfactorily housed, clothed and fed;
— to recognise the financial resources we shall need to live together in physical comfort;
— to express the ways in which each of us tries to care for our physical health; and to identify how our marriage may affect these attitudes and activities;
— to talk realistically about the way physical handicap might affect our marriage and expectations of family life and (when either or both is handicapped) the extent to which we both acknowledge and cope with the nature of the present handicap.

Emotional

— to share with each other the anxieties and misgivings we each may have about being married;
— to acknowledge the effect that being married will have on the attachment each of us has to our own families, and to

talk about the feelings we have about each other's family;
— to recognise how each of us is accustomed to give and
   express love and to respond to affection in an intimate
   relationship;
— to learn about how we are likely to have to change as our
   relationship deepens and how we may learn to deal with
   those changes;
— to share how each of us consciously deals with guilt,
   anger and emotions we find uncomfortable, and how the
   other perceives our behaviour.

Intellectual
— to discuss our ideas about marriage, and our understanding of what each of us is hoping for in our continuing
   relationship;
— to consider differences and similarities in the ways each
   of us deals with matters of planning or problems to be
   solved, and how these are determining our approach to
   married life together;
— to share the ways in which each of us separately and
   together looks for intellectual stimulus and fulfils artistic
   and creative talent; to consider how our marriage might
   affect these interests;
— to learn something about the view of marriage expressed
   in the marriage rite.

Social
— to talk about the effect that being married will have on
   relationships we have with other people and on our
   recreational and social life;
— to look at the way we are arranging our wedding as a
   social event and how this reflects differences and
   similarities in our social background;
— to examine the social conventions that each of us regards
   as important and to consider how these have affected our
   relationship;
— to consider how being married will affect our opportunities
   to find social companionship at work and in the
   neighbourhood of our home;

— to share and discuss our expectations about having children and becoming parents;
— to become more aware of the different roles in which each of us instinctively feels comfortable when belonging to a family or established social group and to relate this to the way we behave as partners.

Sexual
— to use the experience each of us has of sexual relationships to help us discover the needs and expectations that will pattern our sex life;
— to talk about those sex matters that give us anxiety as we approach marriage and discover whether we need to seek further advice to resolve our disquiet and deal with any particular matter;
— to learn about each other's bodies and feelings so that we understand how to treat each other physically and can respect and respond to each other's wishes;
— to consider the implications of any contraceptive method we choose together;
— to examine the assumptions each of us may have about how our roles in marriage and sexual activity relate to our being male or female, husband or wife.

Spiritual
— to learn something about the meaning of marriage as it is expressed by the marriage service;
— to consider our reason for choosing to be married in church and recognise whether we differ in our concern for this;
— to discover the importance each of us attaches to religious belief and Christian practice, particularly those matters on which we have strongly held convictions which we will need to acknowledge in each other;
— to learn about ways in which religious faith can help us to deepen and sustain our marriage;
— to consider how we can both grow in spirit and in our capacity to sustain each other in grief and sadness;

— to recognise how we are able to offer faithfulness to each other in marriage as the means of effecting healing and growth in each other through love.

The matters you consider to be important

Some of the examples listed above might seem to you to be out of place or unrealistic; some you may agree with. While such reactions are fresh in your mind it may be useful to take notes about the issues you consider to be important and would expect many couples to recognise.

Themes and Resources (A Workbook)

1. Roles and Gender

People bring to marriage assumptions about the way men and women behave, or are expected to behave, because they are male or female. Certain qualities or kinds of behaviour may be associated in a person's mind with either being a man or being a woman.

"This is not the typing-pool, Miss Watson. You're a man now and men don't cry."

Upbringing and cultural influences, have helped to shape these perceptions. As individuals we may resist or challenge these influences, because we are not comfortable about conforming to them or wish to be different and assert our own feelings. I may for example be very attracted to the way my intended spouse behaves differently in some respects from members of my family. Social relations provide the opportunity for me to see that all men do not act in the same way, nor do all women. During courtship I have probably recognised that my partner is different and more attractive to me than other members of his or her sex. I will be aware to some degree, although I may not be able to articulate it, that I am more comfortable with some men or women than others.

| Resource 1.1 | *Personal Qualities Checksheet*

It is possible to explore perceptions of gender by learning from our own observations of how men and women behave, and how we think or feel that they ought to behave if we are to be comfortable with them. This theme can provide a basis for conjoint discussion and group activity. The 'Personal Qualities Checksheet' opposite needs to be adapted to suit each setting.

In column 1 of the Checksheet put an M or an F beside any qualities you think of as being especially male or female. If you think they are equally male or female, leave the space blank. Don't show your list to your partner yet.

Complete column 2 by putting your partner's initial opposite each of the qualities you see very clearly in them.

When you have both had time to do this carefully, show each other your completed Checksheets.

Notes for leaders
If the Checksheet is used as part of a group activity it may be appropriate to ask participants to share what they have marked in column 1 with someone else of their own sex, before completing column 2 and talking about that with their partner.

	Column 1	Column 2
	M or F	Partner's Initial
Hardworking		
Cheerful		
Rational		
Strong		
Loyal		
Artistic		
Affectionate		
Dependable		
Funny		
Practical		
Sociable		
Religious		
Emotional		
Talkative		
Good with figures		
Inventive		
Organized		
Tidy		
Clothes conscious		
*		
*		

* *Use these blank spaces to add any qualities not on the list that you usually associate with the opposite sex.*

When using the Checksheet in a conjoint interview, the minister can encourage each partner to share in turn their understanding of what they have marked.

Some additional prompts may be useful:

How does the way you see each other fit your own picture of what it means to be male and female?

Do you want to ask your partner what they meant by anything they wrote down that you do not understand? For example, a quality they have ascribed to you that you do not think you have.

After responding to comments and questions it may be appropriate to suggest that when partners who are married or engaged see each other in a different light or behave in a way that takes them by surprise, their reactions may have something to do with these images they have of gender, e.g. a woman who suddenly takes charge, or a man who admits he can't do something, may cause amazement, delight or irritation.

| Resource 1.2 | *Who Does What?*

Do you assume that husbands do certain jobs because they are men and wives have other tasks because they are women? These assumptions may have been formed by what we are used to at home but they may be challenged at some point through personal experience. For example, when as a child I visit my aunt and uncle, I may find they do things differently from my parents. If in fact I live with just one of my parents, I may notice differences when I see how a couple live together. (Children are natural social researchers; they observe different marriage patterns as they spend time in their friends' houses.) Later on in my own marriage I will discover my spouse's expectations of me as husband or wife. Roles in a marriage are often reinforced in single-sex company: a husband in male company may find his own assumptions strengthened by like-minded friends. Sometimes assumptions are challenged: a wife chatting with other wives may discover that her spouse's way of behaving as a husband is unusual compared with the others she is hearing about.

"Look where you're going. . .Watch out!"

The following resource can be used in group work or conjoint activity with necessary adaptation. The list of role statements has been based in part on material published in *Social Trends 1987* (Table A2 Household Divisions of Labour, by Martin Straker, page 14) HMSO 1987. When preparing your own list think about who will be using it and produce material that will make sense to them. The statements chosen do not have to be opposites; some may be the same for both sexes. There should be an equal number for husbands and wives and they should be clear and unambiguous. Each separate statement is written on a piece of coloured card — a different colour for each sex.

List of Statements for Household Tasks

Colour A	Colour B
WIFE	HUSBAND

looks after the household money and pays the bills	earns the family income
cleans the house	sees to all the repair work on the house
looks after the children when they are sick	teaches the children discipline
does the household shopping	cooks the evening meal
does the washing and ironing	remembers family anniversaries and birthdays
buys clothes for all the family	buys household gadgets and equipment
keeps the fun and affection alive in their marriage	sorts out the problems and crises
Washes up after meals	arranges holidays and leisure activities

If this is a group activity, divide into single-sex groups of men and women. Give to the women a set of 'wife' role cards and to the men a set of 'husband' role cards. Ask each group to sit in a circle, with a set of cards piled in the centre with the printed statements face down. Ask one person in the group to begin by picking up the top card and reading aloud the statement printed on it. Ask them to repeat it after a moment and then ask each person to think about whether they agree or disagree with the statement and record the votes. Continue with the next person on the left taking and reading aloud the second card. After the vote, allow time for discussion about the statements when it arises spontaneously. When the pack has been exhausted, collect all the cards, ensure they are all face down in a pile and exchange the 'husband' and 'wife' sets between groups. Repeat the routine so that the women decide on the 'husband' role and *vice versa*, again recording the votes. Reassemble as one large group; suggest that partners now sit together for this final stage. Read out the results of the voting to the whole group and allow general discussion to follow. If participants are sitting as couples, ask them to discuss their reactions together.

Some participants may wish to insist that in their experience some roles are not exercised by one spouse alone but shared. They may want to record their vote on that basis. It is worth resisting this idea unless it can be clearly established that 'sharing' really means *joint responsibility* (50:50, or as near as 40:60). People may be unwilling to recognise that what they call sharing usually means in practice that one partner may sometimes *give help*, but that in default the other partner has to exercise the role (nearer 90:10 sharing).

2. Values and Money

People's personal convictions and deepest beliefs are often unspoken and only become apparent in the course of major incidents or events in their lives. Yet these convictions and beliefs are ingrained in mundane behaviour that can prove very resistant to change. One way of seeing a link between what we believe deep down and what we value or want most, is to observe the way we spend our money. Arrangements about money may show whether we adopt long-term or short-term aims. Arguments about money will often be a battle in defence of values which may be unconscious and unrealised. So destructive may the battle become, that partners have to agree a truce. When for example money is short, a working agreement about how much is spent on different items may be necessary, although this will be only a partial settlement if partners are unwilling to declare their values or interests.

Before marriage, discussion of money matters can be a means to an end rather than an end in itself. Some couples may need advice on organising their financial affairs but it has to be recognised that a basic inability to handle money is not going to be changed by simple instruction; often personal instability is a cause of financial problems. In the last decade there has been a large increase in the amount of consumer credit offered and owed and many of those marrying today will have very different expectations about what they need and want than their parents did.

Among couples getting married, there will be much variation in the amount of income they will receive and the degree of financial support they will get from their families. Practical exercises involving budgeting will be ineffective if the material used and the information provided does not seem realistic to the couples taking part. The main object of the following exercise is to help couples improve their skill at making decisions on matters deeply affected by their own values and attitudes, it is not a blueprint for monthly cash flow management.

Resource 2.1 Spending Plan

The Spending Plan opposite is designed for use in conjoint discussions but could be adapted for use in a group activity by allowing extra stages for exchanges in pairs and group discussion.

Ask both partners to imagine they are living alone and earning £110 a week after tax. On the Spending Plan which each is given they should divide up the weekly income under the various headings shown. Some columns are left blank so

AMOUNT SPENT ON

	MYSELF					OTHER PEOPLE
	Clothes/ cosmetics/ luxuries	Rent/ Mortgage heat/light rates and maintenance	Food	Entertainment/ Sport/ holidays	Travel inc. car etc.	Presents, hospitality, charities etc
1. £110 per week						
Spend						
Save						
2. £180 per week						
Spend						
Save						
3. Ours £180 p.w.						
Spend						
Save						

they can fill in their own headings. First use line 1 across the columns and write in rough figures. Above the dotted line they put the amount they would expect to spend in a week and below the dotted line the amount they could save to pay for something later.

Next they show each other their spending plan, one at a time; they ask each other questions, but do not try to persuade each other to change.

Now ask them to imagine they are married and their combined income after tax is £180 per week. Each of them on their own reckons how they would divide up that income using the same columns. (Read 'MYSELF' as 'US'.) Assume that they have no debts to pay off. They write their figures on line 2. Then they share with each other what they have allocated under each heading. Again they ask questions and listen to each other's ideas. They look again at line 2 and tick any amounts they would like to increase and put a cross by those they would like to reduce before together agreeing on how they can allocate their weekly money. Discuss how they can revise the figures together and write agreed amounts in line 3 on each of their sheets. Then they look back at their own sheets and consider whether they have had to agree to a priority for spending that they basically feel dissatisfied with.

Ask them to talk together about their choices. If they both agree on the priorities, what might prevent them acting on them? Would they prefer to have separate accounts each or to run a joint account? If they find that they have different priorities do they need to learn more about why each of them thinks and feels the way they do?

3. Communicating Feelings and Affection

It may be appropriate to trigger off conversation deliberately between partners about the affective dimension of their relationship. How does each express feelings and how comfortable are they with each other's ways of doing so? How much does each appreciate or dislike the way the other communicates with them? The following are examples of a work sheet and a set of cards which can be used to prompt self-awareness and conversation.

Resource 3.1 *Dealing with Feelings—His and Hers*

The sample questionnaire below is printed on two sides of an A5 sheet of paper or card. It has been designed so that couples can use side one possibly during an interview . Side two will require additional time together, either in a later session or voluntarily when they are alone together. It may be appropriate in some contexts to use side two straightaway if couples already show a capacity to express and acknowledge feelings.

Side One:

What do I do when I am happy? . . . .

How do I know when you are happy? . . . .

What do I do when I am sad? . . . .

How do I know when you are sad? . . . .

What do I do when I am angry? . . . .

How do I know when you are angry? . . . .

Side Two:

What feelings do I find it hard to express to you? . . . .

What feelings do I wish you could express to me? . . . .

Are there ways I behave that I know you don't like? . . . .

Are there ways you behave I wish you would change? . . . .

What makes me think I can change? . . . .

What makes me think you can change? . . . .

| Resource 3.2 | *Giving and Receiving Affection*

The object of this exercise is to help two partners to recognise things they may want to say to each other about the way they give and receive affection (cf 'to learn about each other's feelings so that each can understand how to treat the other and respect and respond to their wishes', from one of the aims listed in Appendix A).

The questions in the boxes opposite are printed on one side only of ten cards, and the two sets of five cards arranged in this order are placed with the words face down within reach of each partner. The minister invites them to take one card each (to ensure that the exercise is not rushed the minister maintains the pace of the activity by saying when to select each card). In practice much will depend on how willing the partners are to share their thoughts with each other. After they have read and thought about the question on the card they can write down their thoughts or tell them to each other.

This activity is usually more feasible in a group where the number present and the general noise will create a measure of privacy for each pair. Whatever is shared during the exercise, there will be more for couples to talk about later in private.

HIS

HERS

Can you think of
one way your partner
shows affection to
you physically?
Do you like it?

Can you think of
one way your partner
shows affection to
you physically?
Do you like it?

Can you think of
one way you show
affection to your
partner?
Do you know if
she likes it?

Can you think of
one way you show
affection to your
partner?
Do you know if
he likes it?

Does either of you
use words to show
affection?
Think of examples

Does either of you
use words to show
affection?
Think of examples.

Is there one thing
you want to tell
your partner about,
that is something
she does to you
that you dislike
or find unkind?

Is there one thing
you want to tell
your partner about,
that is something
he does to you
that you dislike
or find unkind?

Is there one thing
you want to say to
her today to show
your affection?

Is there one thing
you want to say to
him today to show
your affection?

4. Decision and Conflict

Conflict is a common feature of marriage, yet it is something many partners may not be prepared for or want to deal with. The issue is not *if* we have disagreements, but *when*. They can arise quite simply because spouses come from different family backgrounds, have learned different patterns of domestic behaviour, and remain attached to family ways and loyalties. Men and women, husbands and wives, by gender and by role may be disposed to view an issue or a problem from different standpoints. Difficult domestic circumstances, cramped accommodation or sparse finances will create pressures on the couple and force practical decisions on them. Living together under one roof makes some conflict unavoidable. The failure of one of the spouses to meet the other's expectations can cause irritation which becomes a deepening disappointment, leading to conflict triggered off by domestic incidents.

Much ordinary learned behaviour is a matter of 'win or lose', yet in marriage consensus and compromise are often needed. Many of the primary reasons for conflict in marriage stem from disagreement. Little arguments grow: disagreements over how to treat children, budgeting for expenses and bills, visiting in-laws, housekeeping money, husbands not sharing in domestic chores, wife wanting to get a job, what to do for leisure (including TV watching); in addition the feelings of a wife not being appreciated by a husband, and jealousy of other men or women sometimes assume comparable importance. (Topics like this appear in a survey described in Argyle, M., and Henderson, M., *The Anatomy of Relationships*, Penguin 1985.)

Conflict can be controlled in a day-to-day way by courtesy, convention and careful communication. The obvious courtesies include: respecting each other's privacy and personal status; keeping confidences and maintaining trust; refraining from public criticism and abuse; and maintaining reliability as a partner. Communication will include conversation, the expression of affection, and the mutual enjoyment of sexual play.

Couples who deliberately set aside conventions may enjoy

doing so together publicly. Spectators may be amused by the couple who enjoy banter with each other but what is not amusing is the spectre of conflict in marriage and family life which is emotionally harmful and physically violent, the eruption of deep and often uncontrollable feelings. Such conflict is often caused by unresolved inner personal conflicts which spouses bring to their marriage.

Some marriages for all their stormy appearance actually make life generally tolerable for the partners concerned. A couple may have been drawn to each other and become married through an unconscious process by which they seek to contain unresolved conflicts within themselves. Even when there is a comfortable match, it is still necessary for spouses to develop appropriate behaviour for dealing together with conflict, as too with the negative feelings that are engendered simply by being together (see Resource 3.1). At a basic level both partners need to make time to communicate well with each other, and avoid outright aggression towards one another, learning instead how to be assertive through effective communication. When strong feelings and convictions are expressed, each spouse will need to be able to listen to the other's point of view and try to understand it, both prepared to give way and to try to find a solution by working together.

A routine for handling conflict can be learnt, but it will often require people to modify their instinctive behaviour. A conscious effort to change personal behaviour can be made when two people are ordinarily good at communicating with each other and are sufficiently attached to one another to want to make the effort. Where such conditions do not exist, the activities that are now suggested will not be appropriate.

| Resource 4.1 | *Experience of Decision-Making*

This is a theme that can be explored during a conjoint interview with the minister prompting recollection and discussion. It may arise during a conversation about a couple's courtship story (see chapter 6).

There are often jokes in wedding speeches about the way married couples share the decision-making in their marriage. The man takes all the big decisions such as which bank to use, when to mow the lawn, repair the front gate and service the car and the woman takes all the small decisions like having children, the choice of a house and where to go for a holiday. Quite often though couples never consciously decide who decides what; a pattern simply evolves as they go along. Arguments may be avoided if each partner is boss in their own domain, but in practice it can often be unsatisfactory to divide matters up like that. Decisions may have to be made on the spot by one partner and not deferred until the other one is available. Taking decisions together can be a way of learning each other's views and making it easier for one partner to act for both.

To begin with, partners can be asked to think about their own experience: who decided what, as far as they were aware, at home? Further questions may prompt thoughts about how as individuals they prefer to arrive at decisions.

'What is your own experience of deciding things? As individuals would you say you were thoughtful before deciding something or quick and impulsive in the way you act?'

'Do you like discussing things or do you prefer to reach your decision alone?'

Ask each partner separately to recall an occasion when they had to make a decision about something as a couple. Check that each remembers the occasion that the other has thought of. Using their recollection of both occasions develop a conversation which highlights one or more of the following:

(a) each partner's individually preferred approach to making ordinary decisions;
(b) obvious differences in their individual approaches;
(c) recognisable patterns the couple have developed for dealing with decisions;
(d) any areas in which one or both partners are not satisfied with the way decisions have been made.

If there is an occasion that stands out as memorable for both partners which involved a difficult decision and possibly an argument it may be appropriate to use the following set of questions as a prompt list for recollecting the occasion and learning from what took place. A few of these questions will probably be appropriate, with others suggesting supplementary possibilities.

Checksheet: Analysing a Decision-making Process
What was the main issue or problem from your point of view?
How did the issue arise?
How was the issue resolved?

Did one of you make a particular effort:
— by getting both of you to discuss it?
— by putting forward your personal views?
— by changing your views?
— by suggesting a way you could agree?
— by giving in to your partner's views?

Did one of you:
— try to avoid discussing the issue?
— try to make the decision without consulting the other?
— regret the way you dealt with the issue?

Each partner is encouraged to think of answers in silence (though if they are absorbed and enjoying the exercise there may be quite a bit of laughter or expression). Only a few questions should be asked. If the couple do not begin to respond by developing their answers, the exercise should not be prolonged by asking more questions. The pace at which they share their recollections and the answers to the questions should be such that neither partner is forced to say more than they wish but the minister should ensure they both get equal attention. They may want to discuss their answers and feelings about the exercise.

Because this activity may have caused the couple to be aware of difficulties in their relationship the minister will need to conclude it carefully. The partners will probably have plenty to go away with and talk about and they may wish to know that they can make another appointment to see him to talk more. The exercise is not meant to focus on particular problems but to encourage the couple to learn how to be more effective in decision-making.

5. Further Themes

There are two themes that underlie some of those already described, which can be treated more explicitly.

Sexuality

The minister's knowledge and feelings about sex and particularly sexual intercourse will affect his work with couples even when it is assumed or apparent that the partners themselves are not expecting or wanting sex instruction. Being able to talk in a natural non-clinical way about how lovers use their bodies will help a minister to respond without embarrassment when sexual matters arise in conversation.

The following are examples of published resources which may help a minister to be more sure of what he knows and better able to communicate information to others.

Sexual Response Quiz published as Exercise 15 in *Sharing* (a handbook for those involved in training in personal relationships and sexuality) by Beryl Heather, Family Planning Association Education Unit, 27–35 Mortimer Street, London W1N 7RJ, 1984.

Sex and Life by Brian Ward. Macdonald Educational Ltd. 1976. A well-illustrated, straightforward introduction to the facts of life for adolescents.

Sex Matters published by Yorkshire Television. An educational video tape containing six programmes originally broadcast in 1984, each lasting forty-five minutes. Suitable in a selective way for use with older adolescents and adults.

Sexuality and Communication by Noam and Beryl Chernick, two Canadian therapists and sex counsellors who talk about marital relations and doctor/patient relations and illustrate matters with role play. This fifty-minute film/video tape is available for hire or purchase from Concord Film Council, 201 Felixstowe Road, Ipswich, Suffolk IP3 9BJ. Appropriate for training work with adults intending to discuss sexual behaviour.

Enjoying Sex to the Full is a video-recorded talk in the *Side-by-Side* Marriage Preparation Course published by the Church Pastoral Aid Society, specifically designed for viewing by engaged couples.

Embodiment: an Approach to Sexuality and Christian Theology by James Nelson, SPCK 1978. A thorough study of the way sexuality is dealt with in Christian thought.

Family

Two of the interview illustrations given in chapter 5 referred to family background. This is an obvious theme to explore in other ways, with the primary object of helping partners to recognise how their life and experience in family has already given shape to their personalities and expectations.

Exploring Your Family Story by Douglas Purnell, Joint Board of Christian Education, Melbourne, 1983 (Span Series) is a useful compendium of ideas and outlines including exercises on family story, family time line, and roles, rules and power in families.

Family Policy Studies Centre (231 Baker Street, London NW1 6HS), publish an annual bulletin, a number of carefully researched discussion papers and occasional papers, and a series of fact sheets. A good up-to-date source of information on family patterns.

The Family of the Eighties, Social Workers Christian Fellowship, c/o Mrs P. J. Dale, 20 Harcourt Road, London N22 4XW, contains valuable papers by John Wesson and Jean Wesson and Case Study Material by Claire Wendalken.

The Family, Politics and Social Theory by D. H. J. Morgan, Routledge & Kegan Paul 1985. An academic text for a person interested in relating the institution of marriage to contemporary theories about family and the serious public issues that arise.

Further publications are listed in the Bibliography in Appendix F. Family Life Education is now becoming a recognised concern, supported within the Church of England by the Family Life Education Advisory Group, within the Roman Catholic Church in England and Wales by the Committee for Marriage and Family Life of the Bishops' Conference, and ecumenically by the Family Life Education Ecumenical Project.

6. Further general resources

Some of these items are also listed in the Bibliography, Appendix F.

Marriage Preparation Courses

Your Future Begins Now 2 Volumes. Catholic Marriage Advisory Council, 1984. From CMAC, Clitherow House, 1 Blythe Mews, Blythe Road, London W14 0NW.

A Marriage Preparation Course by Margaret Stevens, 1986, from 5 St Michael's Square, Bramcote, Beeston, Notts, NG9 3HG.

Side by Side by the Church Pastoral Aid Society, 1985. The material includes two video films but of particular interest is the handbook and accompanying worksheets. From CPAS, Falcon Court, 32 Fleet Street, London EC1Y 1DB.

Water Made Wine by Margaret Grimer, Darton, Longman and Todd 1986. An approach based on experience of leading and developing Catholic parish marriage preparation teams.

Preparing for Marriage. A course for engaged couples published by the Family Life Education Ecumenical Project (NE) and obtainable from the North East Institute for Christian Education, Carter House, Pelaw Leazes Lane, Durham, DH1 1TB.

Learning about Relationships

The Anatomy of Relationships by Argyle, M., and Henderson,

M., Penguin Books 1985 and *Human Relationships* by Duck, S., Sage 1986. Each of these two books provides material from the perspective of social psychology which will inform and help people to conceptualise. The information can be adapted and used for exercises and discussion.

Lifeskills: Teaching Programmes by Hopson, B., and Scally, M. Three files of worksheets designed for use in group work with adolescents and adults.

Building Relationships, Family Relationships and *Marriage Relationships* by Grigor, J. C., (Connections Series), Bible Society 1986/87. Designed for discussion groups.

Making Relationships Work by Sandford, C., and Beardsley, W., Sheldon Press 1986. Deals particularly with work with couples based on marriage guidance counselling. A good basic chapter on marital interaction.

7. Audio Visual Aids

The interaction between minister and couple is at the heart of the learning process and elaborate resources that are not carefully used can intrude on this interaction or displace it. Audio tapes are of limited value except when an excerpt of short duration is used to trigger recognition or is specifically related to an issue or experience already identified as significant. Listening to talks on tape, however good they are, has an inhibiting effect on people sitting in company and can prevent relaxed discussion. Audio tapes may be more useful as a back-up for ministerial or leader training, or for individual listening. A useful set is contained in *Marriage Preparation: a practical programme of pre-marriage instruction*, Redemptorist Publications 1981, Alphonse House, Chawton, Alton, Hants GU34 3HQ.

Visual aids can be very simple and are often more immediate in their effect: photographs and cartoons mounted on card can be useful for helping people to recall personal experience or identify with particular situations. Slides may be used for this too, provided they can be projected without fuss. Video recordings are easier to show than reels of film and there are an increasing number of instructional videos available, but they need to be used carefully. Most video cassettes currently obtainable are largely didactic and rely a great deal on 'talking heads'. Video films can be especially useful to trigger responses and to encourage recollection or highlight genuine experience. Extracts shown to a relaxed and properly prepared group can be very useful in consciousness raising and discussion. The person using them has to be thoroughly conversant with the extract to be used and be able to assess audience reaction. Trigger extracts usually last about six minutes and become ineffective for that purpose if they are longer than ten minutes. The short showing is designed to produce immediate and sharp reaction. Longer extracts lasting up to twenty minutes may be useful at a stage when a group is learning about social skills and would benefit from a short observation exercise. A longer instructional film would only be appropriate if it were clear that participants needed and wanted such instruction and were able to deal with it critically afterwards.

Leaders and ministers who want to use short film extracts may find that the best source will be their own recording off-air used privately. In this country a Channel 4 licensing scheme is already in operation which allows for the legitimate copying of some films for training purposes. Hired feature films can also be useful. The *Side by Side* marriage preparation programmes referred to above (p. 148) includes two video cassettes providing instructional talks and discussion starters. The Churches' Television Centre has produced *Great Expectations?* (CTVC, Beesons Yard, Bury Lane, Rickmansworth, Herts WD3 1DS) which is useful for training purposes.

Those with access to portable video cameras may find they have a useful means of observing and recording people's actions in training and this is a useful way of bringing locally recorded interviews into pre-marriage discussion work. Where churches make arrangements to allow couples to have their own weddings recorded they may find it especially appropriate to make sensitive use of locally recorded material. The inherent danger in making use of any film material is that people watching it can easily slip from being participants learning from experience to spectators simply being entertained.

The Decision to Marry in Particular Circumstances

Rising divorce rates have encouraged research into some of the factors that put marriages particularly at risk. Some of these are clearly social and physical and are related to housing difficulties, acute financial hardship and health problems. It is also clear that certain personal factors can increase the probability of marriage breakdown.

Marrying young

Recent research in England (see, for example, Kiernan, K. E., 'Teenage marriage and marital breakdown: a longitudinal study' (*Population Studies* 40, no. 1, 1986)) has shown the significantly high incidence of early marriage breakdown among those who marry as teenagers. Ministers may therefore be concerned to recognise and respond to clues that a young couple, in particular, are embarking upon an unstable marriage.

The following factors are likely to be significant in this respect:

(a) *Emotional immaturity.* A person who is in some respects still a child may be looking for a parent with whom to continue growing up. Their partner is, for the moment, fulfilling that role, but when the 'child' grows up may no longer be needed for it. If there is no potential for adaptation when different roles are eventually needed, disenchantment is likely.

(b) *Wanting to get better.* A person who has been deeply hurt, or who feels worthless, may be glad to be with someone who makes them well, affirms them and wants them. Such a partner offers hope of change and healing and the relationship may become deeply affected by personal gratitude for what each has given the other. Those who marry young may be searching for a healing relationship and yet both partners may be insufficiently mature to sustain what is needed.

(c) *Gaining status.* Marriage has in different ways given individuals and couples a respectable status. A person who views marriage in this way may marry prematurely in order to gain a status that has eluded him or her, or to acquire a reputation for normality by conforming to popular expectations. For some people a wife or a husband may be useful for professional or social reasons and while not necessarily marrying young they may do so impersonally, paying disproportionate attention to social or financial incentives.

(d) *Becoming adult.* It is still true that most people live with their families until they marry and may have no other option. Young adults who are treated as children at home, who are exploited or are enmeshed in restrictive relationships, may find an escape route in marriage. Marrying then provides a means to an end which may quickly achieve its object — the transition from adolescent subordination to adult independence. If the marriage relationship in turn becomes restrictive, another escape route will be needed. Escaping can become a habit.

When a couple are marrying young, one of the partners may be partly aware of an underlying factor such as those we have mentioned and the way it has influenced the process of seeking marriage. The minister's task is to help both partners to recognise those unconscious factors which are evident to him as an outsider, so that the couple may consider them safely. One partner may need the security provided by the conversation with the minister to reconsider the decision to marry and to end a relationship in which he or she has become unwittingly enmeshed. It is however worth stressing again that young marriage is not of itself the problem; it is the presence of one or more of the factors referred to, that can create problems later for those who marry young. In fact, in this country there is a trend away from marrying young.

Mixed marriages

When two partners are firmly committed to practising different faiths or come from distinctively different backgrounds and cultures, they will soon be aware of the conflicts that can arise in their day-to-day behaviour. When they accept one another and affirm one another with these differences, the effort made to embrace each other's convictions can have a profound and gracious effect on their marriage. It is often not the partners themselves but those with whom they have contact, who complicate life for couples involved in a mixed marriage. Family, friends and ministers, instead of acknowledging the union and supporting the couple as they grow together, may convey the attitude that they are making a bad match or make inappropriate demands on the respective loyalties of the partners. The problem therefore is often not with the marriage itself but with the way others choose to behave towards the couple and the way they treat their marriage.

An obvious case for ministers to face is the experience of those who marry with different denominational allegiances. A useful distinction can be made between those technically mixed marriages in which both partners are nominally affiliated to different Churches through family background, and interchurch marriages in which both partners are practising church members. The Association of Interchurch Families has done a great deal to inform and support couples. Members of the Association locally may be helpful contacts for ministers working with interchurch couples. The AIF has published a 'Centrepiece' article, 'Getting Married', in its newsletter, which is still obtainable and which may be useful to give to couples.

Couples who are together trying to maintain a double allegiance often refer to themselves as 'double belonging'. They will have chosen to maintain allegiance to their separate Churches, but in their marriage they will wish to affirm one another's faith, and wish to show this by attending worship in one another's churches. They will also want to worship together for their own sake and participate as fully as possible in the life of both churches as a recognised couple. Up and down the country, couples attempting this faithfulness in marriage, will experience different reactions from their families, friends and clergy. Parents will often put pressure on their offspring and they may be less tolerant of another Church's discipline than their children are. In most cases involving weddings and baptisms, the couple will have to talk with two ministers. Sometimes the ministers will make it easier for the couple by meeting together with them, but often ecumenical relationships will not be sufficiently developed or confident enough for this to be considered. For one minister to make a unilateral decision may be unhelpful, even when, as is often the case, it is the discipline of one Church or the attitudes of its local minister that appear to be the main problem.

Inter-faith and cross-cultural marriages involve consideration of ethnic issues. There is a valuable appendix about some of the matters that need considering in Hooker, R., and Lamb, C., *Love the Stranger*, SPCK 1986.

Marrying again

A person previously married may become attracted to a new partner, and may also wish to marry again. This may happen despite still unhappy memories of a previous marriage or the untimely ending of a happy one: to be married again may offer relief from sadness and from the loneliness of being unmarried. People who have been married once have shown that they are disposed to marry; experience may caution them against a hasty decision to repeat marriage but time and attachment may overcome caution. There will be those for whom there can be no intention of a second marriage, whether it is because they are still attached to their former partner, or because to marry again would be against their personal convictions, or because the first experience taught them that they are not willing and able to commit themselves to all that marriage entails. Those who decide to marry again will probably face some problems and demands that did not arise when they married for the first time. There may be continuing commitments that are consequences of a first marriage (for example maintenance, mortgage payments, care and control of children, relationships with former parents-in-law and mutual friends). Such matters can be satisfactorily dealt with but often they are not properly resolved before a new marriage is entered upon. Other demands may be less obvious such as the emotional needs created by bereavement or divorce, or the need to deal with the continuing presence of the former spouse and his or her influence on events.

The breakdown of a marriage is a series of events and even when it has culminated in divorce the partners are unlikely to have dealt with the emotional effect of the experience. When people go through marriage breakdown, separation, divorce, living single and another marriage they may recognise peaks of emotional intensity, both along the way and later. These peaks may be associated with particular occasions: the decision to separate, actual separation, legal divorce, re-marriage of either spouse, death of either spouse and the lifecycle transitions of children. For some people the process may feel like 'a roller coaster ride'. (Carter, E. A., and McGoldrick, M., 'Forming a Remarried Family' in *The Family Life Cycle,* New York: Gardner Press 1980.)

Even though a person may express a lot of grief at the time of a divorce, this will not usually complete the emotional process; but the more that is done at each peak-event, the less intense and disruptive will be the subsequent events. Among the feelings that may have to be dealt with are anger, sadness and confusion. The confusion may be created by the transitoriness of moods — feeling all right one day and deflated the next; ruminating about the past and thinking optimistically about the future; being resolved to manage life and lacking direction. Resolving this confusion may provide the confidence to marry again. Divorce occasions bereavement but without a body to bury. Divorce often proves to be a much more painful process than was ever imagined. Those who have undergone it may be cautious about risking it again and yet know that if divorce ever becomes necessary again they can survive it and will be better at doing so. This is the mentality with which a person may come to a second marriage. It is an event less clearly provided for by established rites of passage.

In the interview process it may help a couple to recognise factors that arise because one of the partners has been married before. There will be other issues as well, no different from those arising in first marriages.

The couple may be reluctant to address the issue of marrying again because it seems one-sided when one partner has not been previously married. Yet the matter is not solely the concern of the previously married partner. It is an inescapable fact, borne out by general experience, that a previous marriage will have an effect on both the partners in the subsequent marriage. This does not mean that the first marriage is itself a problem; the initial task is to encourage the couple to recognise how that past union and its consequences may affect their intended marriage. At some point the couple may realise that if a particular issue is not resolved they will have a problem to deal with, and they may want to discuss that with the minister.

There will be a lot of variations. One couple may recognise the previous marriage to be affecting their relationship even if it is not a topic they find easy to discuss. Another couple may regard a previous marriage as only a legal or historical technicality, ended by divorce some years before the present relationship began. It may have been a union without children that had lasted for only a short time and had been terminated by mutual consent and with mutual relief. As such it would appear to be just a fact of history that does not carry much spiritual or emotional importance any more. Even when the previous marriage does not seem relevant and for the partner concerned has proved to be very empty, it may still be helpful to look at his or her expectations of another marriage, and the significance of marriage vows. There will be many different starting points. The important task for the person conducting the interview is to give the couple themselves the means to elicit important information and to recognise the self-know-ledge that derives from this previous marriage experience.

One way of doing this is to ask questions that will draw out some of the facts and feelings one or other partner may not have recognised or communicated to the other. Questions could be systematically presented as a questionnaire. (An example is given by Fryer, M., in a paper 'Brief Marital Counselling with Second Marriages' in *Relating to Marriage*, National Marriage Guidance Council, 1985.) Where partners have been willing to complete questionnaires of this kind, the activity has often caused distress. Certainly this is not an exercise to embark upon if a minister is not prepared to allow people to recognise and attend to such feelings; when this is necessary and can be done, both partners may be greatly helped in approaching their marriage.

A time-line approach (see chapter 6) may be useful in helping a person to recognise significant events:

When did your partner die? What do you remember doing then?
When do you feel your marriage ended? What caused or led to this occasion?
When did you last see that partner? What were you feeling for them?
When did you meet your new partner? How did your relationship begin?

A person previously married may need to recognise what is left over from that marriage — feelings about the marriage and insights gained from it; feelings about their former partner; continuing relationships with, and responsibilities for, children. A range of useful questions may suggest themselves as the minister helps both partners to recognise the effect a previous marriage will have on their lives together. The following selection of examples shows what questions may be appropriate.

Are you still living in the same house?
What have you done with your husband's things?
What has happened to the mementoes of your marriage?
What are your relationships now with those parents-in-law?

Did your previous partner know the person you now intend to marry?
Would her views still matter to you?

In what ways is your intended spouse like your previous husband?

How does your intended wife differ from your former wife?

Where are you going to live when you are married?

Do you have children from your previous marriage?

Do you and your intended spouse intend to share your home with them?

What does each of your children feel about that and about you marrying again?

Do you both know how each of you regards these continuing responsibilities to the children?

What financial commitments do you have arising out of the previous marriage?

What does each of you think and feel about those?

What do you look forward to in marrying again?

What makes you anxious about marrying again?

In attending to the previous marriage when only one of the partners has been married before, it can be difficult to avoid focusing a lot of attention on that person. Yet the experience of ending a deep relationship or of being bereaved is not just related to a previous marriage. Both partners may be aware of endings and a desire for new beginnings in their life stories and a minister needs to recognise how each partner can identify with the other's experience as well as their own. To provide encouragement and scope for that to happen is an important task.

APPENDIX D

Object-relations Theory

Individuals viewed psychologically can be regarded as growing through a series of phases or stages; these are variously described in different theories. The psychoanalysts Melanie Klein and W. R. D. Fairbairn viewed this developmental process as 'the passage through a succession of positions of conflict and ambivalence'.[1] This psychodynamic view is based on the idea that the whole person (the ego) is developing in the context of interpersonal relations. Fairbairn developed a theory of object-relations to depict 'the strivings and difficulties of the ego (as existing from birth and using instinctual forces) in its endeavour to reach an object where it may find support.'[2] His associates in commenting on this new view recognised a shift away from Freudian theory which emphasises the stimulation of the nervous system by certain instinctive drives to a view in which the instincts are progressively organised by the whole person as it attempts to function satisfactorily.

Attachment and love

In the early months of life the infant (let us say a boy) is dependent on a close attachment figure (let us say his mother) to meet his need for loving attention and care. In the nursing relationship she is part of him and the attachment between them will excite in each of them the need to be loved and to give love. (In this first reciprocal relationship which the child experiences there is an intimation of love in which there is no fear.) Yet mother and child also frustrate and disappoint each other; one will fail to respond to the other's need. Each may experience feelings of rejection; for the child who is utterly dependent on what flows from his mother this is a

160

threat to his survival. (It may stir unconscious memories of rejection in the mother which she needs to deny.) The developing ego of the child will fight off the feelings of rejection in order to survive. He may fear the excitement of love because it is associated with the experience of rejection. He may also fear his own rages if these coincide with the child's being rejected.

To develop as a whole person the child has to learn to bear within himself the force of these contradictory needs and responses, and resolve within himself the conflict they create. The mother by tolerating the child's rages as well as enjoying his loving responses, and by resolving her own feelings of affection and anger towards him will help to achieve this integration of feelings. At the same time he will become aware of his mother's separateness and test out whether she is on balance someone he can trust. He may not always have her attention just when he wants it, but if he can rely on her presence and affection enough for his sense of comfort and well-being, this will be sufficient and the conflict within him will be bearable. He will learn to tolerate the shortcomings and gain mastery of his feelings. Infants will vary in the demands they make, the way in which they resolve these feelings and their patience in testing the reality of mother love. The progressive development of the ego through infancy and childhood is stimulated by the child's experience of reciprocated relations, first with his mother and later with others.

Denial and splitting

As the child begins to differentiate between his own feelings and behaviour and the world around him and recognises that he can experience ambivalent feelings towards his attachment figure, he may start to fear the consequences of what he feels and does. If he gets angry he may jeopardise the relationship; it may no longer be safe to vent his feelings. 'Splitting' is a way of referring to an unconscious adjustment which seems to occur in order to deal with this conflict. Object-relations theory visualises the developing ego as an inner world which consists of images of the self and objects with which the self is in relation. The ego represses the knowledge of these feelings it fears along with the image of the object that excites them. It does this by splitting off the object along with the part of the ego and associated feelings which are invested in the feared object. Objects which excite the love-need (libidinal objects) and objects which deny that need by their rejection (anti-libidinal objects) are equally likely to be split off. As a result the ego becomes differentiated into (i) the conscious part which experiences the mother as a safe and reliable object, neither too exciting nor too denying to cope with (the central ego); and (ii) two split off parts, the libidinal ego and the anti-libidinal ego, which include those aspects of the mother which have become split off and are represented as the libidinal (need-exciting) object and anti-libidinal (need-denying) object.[3]

One of the developmental tasks of the ego is to limit the extent of this splitting and denial, by reintegrating into the central ego the objects that have been repressed along with the ego invested in them. When this splitting off has been maintained from early in childhood, a great deal of the relational potential the person may have had becomes bound up with defending the ego from the threat of feared objects. Splitting is a defence mechanism present to some degree in all individuals; it might be compared to the way in which the human body threatened by cold survives by maintaining body heat in its central core and reducing the flow of blood to the surface skin, arms and legs.

Continuing development

Early parental acceptance is a child's first lesson in adult love and if the experience becomes an integral part of his sense of reality, it provides an internal resource he can begin to use and learn to trust as he makes relations with other people. It is this capacity for making attachments that is developed or inhibited through developmental experience and in due course affects the process of making and sustaining other intimate relationships. In any home parental support may not always offer (for a variety of reasons) sufficient acceptance and toleration to provide a child with adequate 'objects-relations' within which to resolve the conflicts he experiences. This will be particularly true if parents engaged in their own intense conflicts communicated a great deal more rejection than love to their children.

There are a series of developmental phases through childhood and adolescence. The oedipal stage is so called because it marks the emergence of fantasy feelings of sexual rivalry between the child and one parent with corresponding sexual attraction towards the other. When the father and the mother are clearly united and co-operating in caring for the child, they provide securely related objects which will resist any fantasy desire in the child to drive them apart and replace one of them as partner. On the other hand, violence between parents and the frustration of sexual relations between them encourages the child's fantasy. These fantasy feelings will be further heightened if the child is actually subjected to hateful rejection or erotic affection from one or other parent. In a healthy development the child is encouraged to realise that these oedipal fantasies are futile.

This is a prolonged stage of development which provides recurring opportunity for a child to experience identification with each parent in turn. If parents for their part cope well with the alternating loyalty and rejection which the child expresses towards them, they provide the security the child needs to begin to differentiate the maternal and paternal roles, the male and female. By this phase the child is aware of being a boy or a girl, an awareness which is supported by physical evidence and empathy with the actual behaviour of parents. The child will have formed inner mother and father objects and will also have incorporated the role behaviour associated with each in its own self-image. Both objects provide internal role models, prototypes of the child's father-like and mother-like potentials. Here is 'an inner blue-print of a complete human unit — half oneself, half the love object'.[4] Supported by the reality of the secure parental couple the child is freed to test this sexual identity in the wider world and in relations with siblings and peers.

Notes

1. Dicks, H., *Marital Tensions*, Routledge & Kegan Paul, p. 37.
2. Dicks, H., op. cit., p. 7.
3. I have drawn this account from Dicks, H., op. cit. and Scharff, D., *The Sexual Relationship*, Routledge & Kegan Paul, 1982.
4. Dicks, op. cit., p. 39.

Administration

Whatever the particular circumstances attending the marriage of each couple and the response a minister makes to these, he will need to be systematic in keeping a record of necessary information and the progress of interviews. Where several couples are being dealt with at any season of the year, a flow chart and summary table may be useful. This will mean recognising definite stages in the interview process. The following list is one example of a way of systematically checking the factual details that may have to be dealt with.

Checklist: Obtaining and providing basic information

Enquiry by Couple
Are both partners over sixteen years of age?
IF NOT, advise them of the legal requirements and see if they need more assistance.

Are residence/Electoral Roll qualifications satisfied for at least one partner?
IF YES, arrange first interview.
IF NO, advise or parishes to approach or other action.

First stage
(a) Complete application form:

— Ask for dates of birth: will one of the partners be under eighteen on the wedding day? Ask for written parental consent;
— Is one of the partners a practising Christian of another denomination? Check which Church and take appropriate action;

165

- Is one of the partners not baptised? Are neither of the partners baptised? Where this requires further consideration and action, make a note of it;
- Will either of the partners be moving before wedding? Check on residence/Banns qualifications;
- Is either one of the partners divorced? Check details and any action needed;
- Ask for details of nationality. Is one of the partners a foreign national or a follower of a non-Christian religion? Check action that may be necessary.

(b) Check proposed date and time of wedding; renegotiate if date inconvenient.

(c) Check on provisional wishes with regard to service arrangements: organ, choir, heating, flowers, recording facilities. Give information about costs and answer any other questions.

(d) Explain about the need to arrange for Banns to be called in other parishes or the need to obtain a Superintendent Registrar's Certificate as appropriate.

Second Stage:
(e) Check that arrangements to have Banns called or obtain S.R's certificate have been made.

(f) Present the service options to the couple, outlining the forms and alternatives provided for the Church's marriage rite, and consider their response;
- Where there is a choice of readings or prayers to be made, help the couple to make the choice in their own time together. (Decision may be deferred and given at the rehearsal unless a service order is being printed);
- Help the couple to make a choice of music and hymns that will be suitable: note these details to give the organist, or encourage the couple to meet the organist;
- Discover whether the couple have further requests to make about the service details.

(g) Obtain an estimate of how many people the couple are expecting to come to the service and whether anyone will

need special arrangements for reasons such as disability;
— Note the name of the best man, number of bridesmaids, number of rings being used (one or two), name of person giving the bride away (if appropriate), number of parents who will be present and if any have married again, their present names. (This information is useful when meeting family before the ceremony.)
— Check that the names of each partner are correctly recorded and ask who they will want to sign the register as witnesses.

(h)   Confirm the final amount of money to be paid in fees and make arrangements to receive any necessary payments and documents before the wedding day (possibly at the rehearsal);
— Arrange the time and date of the rehearsal (are others beside the bride and groom invited to be present?).

(i)   Ask the couple for the address where they intend living after they are married; check that they are happy for it to be recorded and consider whether it would be appropriate to commend them to another minister or keep in touch with them.

(j)   Check if there are any other matters about which the couple want to ask.

The Use of a Checklist

I have never sat down with a couple going through those items in exactly this order, but I have found it helpful to keep a check on what has been done at each interview, using such a list as a reminder.

Bibliography

Abrams, M., Gerrard, D., and Timms, N., ed., *Values and Social Change in Britain.* Macmillan 1985.

Alternative Service Book 1980. The Marriage Service.

Anderson, M., 'What is new about the Modern Family: an historical perspective' in *The Family.* Office of Population Censuses and Surveys, Occasional Paper no. 31, 1983.

Archbishop of Canterbury's Commission on the Christian Doctrine of Marriage, *Marriage, Divorce and the Church.* SPCK 1971.

Argyle, M., and Henderson, M., *The Anatomy of Relationships.* Penguin 1985.

Bailey, D. Sherwin, *The Man Woman Relationship in Christian Thought.* Longman 1966.

Baker, J. A., *The Whole Family of God.* Mowbray 1981.

Barker, D. Leonard, 'A Proper Wedding' in M. Corbin, ed., *The Couple.* Penguin 1978.

Bernard, J., *The Future of Marriage.* Souvenir Press 1973.

Book of Common Prayer. The Solemnisation of Matrimony.

Brannen, J., and Collard, J., *Marriages in Trouble: the process of seeking help.* Tavistock 1982.

Bunting, I., *Preaching at Weddings.* Grove Worship Series no. 74 1980.

Carr, W., *Brief Encounters.* SPCK 1985.

Carter, E. A., and McGoldrick, M., *The Family Life Cycle: A Framework for Family Therapy.* New York: Gardner Press, 1980. Chapter 12, 'Forming a Remarried Family.'

Clulow, C. F., 'Children — for better for worse?' in *Change in Marriage.* National Marriage Guidance Council 1982.

Clulow, C. F., *To Have and To Hold.* Aberdeen University Press 1982.

Dicks, H. V., *Marital Tensions*. Routledge & Kegan Paul 1967.

Dod, John and Clever, Robert, *A Godlie Forme of Household Government* 1612.

Dominian, J., *Make or Break*. SPCK 1984.

Dominian, J., *Marriage Faith and Love*. Fount Paperbacks 1984.

Dryden, W., *Marital Therapy in Britain* vols. 1 and 2. Harper and Row 1986.

Duck, S., *Human Relationships*. Sage 1986.

Dunstan, G. R., 'The Marriage Covenant' (*Theology* 78, May 1975).

Efficiency Scrutiny Report on the Registration of Births, Marriages and Deaths. Office of Population Censuses and Surveys 1985.

Fryer, M., 'Brief Marital Counselling with Second Marriages' in *Relating to Marriage*. National Marriage Guidance Council 1985.

Garland, D. S. R., *Working with Couples for Marriage Enrichment*. San Francisco: Jossey-Bass 1983.

'General Household Survey' in *Social Trends 1987*. HMSO.

Gillis, J. R., *For Better, For Worse. British Marriages 1600 to the present*. Oxford University Press 1985.

Gorer, G., *Exploring the English Character*. Cresset Press 1955.

Grigor, J. C., *Building Relationships, Family Relationships*, and *Marriage Relationships*. Bible Society 1986, 1987.

Grimer, M., *Making Marriage Work*. Geoffrey Chapman 1987.

Grimer, M., *Water made Wine*. Darton, Longman and Todd 1986.

Hooker, R. and Lamb, Christopher, *Love the Stranger*. SPCK 1986.

Jacobs, M., *Swift to Hear*. SPCK 1985.

James, A. L., and Wilson, K., *Couples, Conflict and Change*. Tavistock 1986.

Jasper, R. C. D., and Bradshaw, P. F., *A Companion to the Alternative Service Book*. SPCK 1986.

Jowell, R., Witherspoon, S., and Brook, L., *British Social Attitudes: the 1987 Report*. Gower 1987.

Kiernan, K., 'The Structure of Families Today: continuity and change? in *The Family*. OPCS Occasional Paper 31, 1983.

Kindred, M., *Once upon a group*. Privately published 1987.

Leonard, D., *Sex and Generation*. Tavistock 1980.

Mace, D., *Close Companions*. The Marriage Enrichment Handbook. New York: Continuum Books 1984.

Mace, D., and Mace, V., *Love and Anger in Marriage*. Pickering Paperbacks 1983.

Mace, D., and Mace, V., *How to Have a Happy Marriage*. Nashville, NN: Abingdon 1977.

Mansfield, P., 'Motives for Marriage: Romance or Reasons?' Paper read at the International Union of Family Organisations Conference, 'Getting Married Today', Milan, June 1985.

Mansfield, P., *Young People and Marriage*. Scottish Marriage Guidance Council Occasional Paper 1, 1985.

Mansfield, P., and Collard, J., *The Beginning of the Rest of your Life?* Macmillan 1988.

Marriage Matters: A Consultative Document by the Working Party on Marriage Guidance. HMSO 1979.

Marwick, A., *British Society Since 1945*. Pelican 1982.

McFarlane, A., *Marriage and Love in England 1300 to 1840*. Blackwell 1986.

Mitman, John L. C., *Premarital Counselling*. New York: Seabury 1980.

Murgatroyd, S., *Counselling and Helping*. Methuen 1985.

Olson, D. H., 'How Effective is Marriage Preparation?' in Mace, D., ed., *Prevention in Family Services*. Sage 1983.

Open University Community Education Department, *Leading a Group*, Open University 1986.

Perham, M., *Liturgy Pastoral and Parochial*. SPCK 1984.

Phipps, M., 'The Clergy Marriage'. (Westminster Pastoral Foundation Quarterly, Summer 1982).

Reed, B. D., *The Dynamics of Religion*. Darton, Longman and Todd 1978.

Reed, B. D., *Values to Live By: A Study of Dependence*. The Grubb Institute 1985.

Sarsby, J., *Romantic Love and Society*. Penguin 1983.

Scharff, D. E., *The Sexual Relationship*. Routledge & Kegan Paul 1982.

Schillebeeckx, E., *Marriage: Human Reality and Saving Mystery*. Sheed and Ward 1965.

Side by Side. Church Pastoral Aid Society 1985.

Skynner, R., and Cleese, J., *Families and How to Survive Them*. Methuen 1983.

Stahlmann, R. F., and Hiebert, W. J., *Premarital Counselling*. Lexington, MA: Lexington Books 1980.

Stevens, M., *A Marriage Preparation Course*. 1986.

Stevenson, K., *Nuptial Blessing*. Alcuin Club/SPCK 1982.

Tinsley, F. J., *The Imitation of God in Christ*. SCM 1960.

Tinsley, E. J., 'Tell it Slant' (*Theology* 83, May 1980).

Walrond-Skinner, S., *Family Therapy: the treatment of natural systems*. Routledge & Kegan Paul 1976.

Walrond-Skinner, S., *Family Matters: The Pastoral Care of Personal Relationships*. SPCK 1988.

Whitehead, J. D., and Whitehead, E. E., *Marrying Well: Stages on the Journey of Christian Marriage*. New York: Doubleday 1981.

Whitehead, J. D., and Whitehead, E. E., *Method in Ministry*. New York: Seabury 1980.

Your Future Begins Now. Two vols. Catholic Marriage Advisory Council 1984.

Index